WITHDRAWN

The Singing and Acting Handbook

- *The Singing and Acting Handbook* helps the performer to develop the skills required to sing and act at the same time.
- It will strengthen the performer in individual areas such as imagination, spontaneity, awareness, concentration.
- The book looks beyond the separate arts of singing and acting, and helps build up an awareness of how music, text and stage action can combine to form a single powerful expression.
- The exercises explore the co-ordination of rhythm, pulse, pitch, harmony, text, emotional impulse, and characterisation on stage.
- Unique amongst practical handbooks, this volume addresses crucial topics such as the unification of real time and musical time; moving from speech to song; sustaining emotion while singing; and combining free dramatic expression with formalised musical structures.
- It is a long-awaited set of resources for the performer and workshop leader alike.

Thomas de Mallet Burgess works internationally as a freelance director and workshop leader in opera, musicals and spoken theatre. In the UK he has worked for the Royal Opera House, Opera North, Welsh National Opera, the Lyric Theatre Hammersmith, the Guildhall School of Music and Drama and the Royal Academy of Music.

Nicholas Skilbeck works internationally as a musical director, composer, vocal coach and pianist. In the UK he has worked for Cameron Mackintosh as Musical Director of *Cats*, the Lyric Theatre Hammersmith and the Royal National Theatre. He has led workshops in opera and musical theatre for Opera North, the Studio des Variétés in Paris, and the Royal Academy of Music.

The Singing and Acting Handbook

Games and Exercises for the Performer

Thomas de Mallet Burgess
and Nicholas Skilbeck

London and New York

First published 2000
by Routledge
11 New Fetter Lane, London EC4P 4EE

Simultaneously published in the USA and Canada
by Routledge
29 West 35th Street, New York, NY 10001

Routledge is an imprint of the Taylor & Francis Group

Typeset in Janson by Keystroke, Jacaranda Lodge, Wolverhampton
Printed and bound in Great Britain by St Edmundsbury Press,
Bury St Edmunds, Suffolk

British Library Cataloguing in Publication Data
A catalogue record for this book is available from the British Library

Library of Congress Cataloguing in Publication Data
De Mallet Burgess, Thomas, 1964–
    The singing and acting handbook : games and exercises for the
  performer / Thomas De Mallet Burgess and Nicholas Skilbeck.
       p.   cm.
    Includes bibliographical references (p.) and index.
    1. Acting in musical theater. I. Skilbeck, Nicholas, 1965– .
  II. Title.
MT956.D4   1999
792.6'028–dc21   99-29440
                                                            CIP

ISBN 0–415–16657–8 (hbk)
ISBN 0–415–16658–6 (pbk)

To the singing and acting performer

[an artist] stands confident in the storms of spring without the fear that after them may come no summer. It does come. But it comes only to the patient, who are there as though eternity lay before them, so unconcernedly still and wide.

Rainer Maria Rilke, *Letters to a Young Poet*
(translation by M.D. Herter Norton)

Contents

Preface

The Singing and Acting Handbook: Games and Exercises for the Performer began in 1993. We were asked to devise a workshop programme based on Verdi and Boito's opera *Falstaff*. In order to explore this opera we needed exercises that looked at different ways to integrate music and drama. The exercises we had to hand could only take us part of the way. What we specifically lacked were tasks that combined the disciplines of singing and acting. As stage director and musical director we realised that our separate experiences had provoked similar convictions regarding the art of singing and acting in performance. The dialogue began, a singing and acting game was created. Our work has since continued in theatres, opera houses, rehearsal rooms, colleges, conservatories, schools and community centres with performers and students of the performing arts in Britain and many other countries.

The exploratory nature of our research has involved a turmoil of ideas and possibilities. In attempting to find a form and format for clarifying these ideas on paper we are constantly made aware of the hugely complex character of the subject matter in a field that incites the most passionate discord of opinions. In *The Singing and Acting Handbook* we have tried to categorise, streamline and rationalise the results of our exploration to date. The structure that has emerged reflects the particular communication we have established as artists working in a highly collaborative art form. The practical application of our ideas has encouraged performers to further explore their craft. It is the response that we have received which has encouraged us to write this book in the hope that it will be of use to others who are interested in developing this area of theatre.

The book takes an introductory look at the disciplines specifically related to the coming together of singing and acting in performance. It is written for performers interested in understanding the many different factors that may influence the development of their craft as they strive to meet the stringent demands placed upon them when called upon to sing and act at the same time. Further notes are written to benefit the stage director and musical director (including teachers and workshop leaders) who are looking to explore the particular demands of this medium with performers through a combination of practical exercises, observations and discussion. Finally we hope that the book will be of some use to the composers and writers in whose hands the future of sung theatre also lies.

Our central idea is that when music and drama come together through acting, movement, words and music, the result is more than the sum of its constituent parts. While the disciplines and demands in different forms of musical dramatic entertainment (what we term 'sung theatre') are varied and potentially conflicting, they nevertheless involve the coming together of singing and acting in one form or another. Mastering the separate disciplines of singing and acting individually does not automatically lead to mastery of the discipline required to unite them in performance. We believe that the integration of singing and acting is an area of study made necessary by the increasing demands placed on the performer in sung theatre, an area of theatre that is becoming ever more sophisticated and popular. This book is a practical exploration of this ethos.

The exercises, discussion and observations are not intended to represent a fully developed programme of study. Nor are they simply the practice of committing to paper every exercise or game we have used. They are above all a response to a range of challenges that have emerged in rehearsal. Though these exercises can be used as part of the rehearsal process, pressure of time in the rehearsal room allows for only limited exploration. The workshop environment, however, provides the time and space necessary to practise and assimilate. This in turn frees the performer to take advantage of the opportunities encountered in the rehearsal room.

Many of the games and exercises in this book have been invented by us. Others have been adapted from the wide pool of material shared and handed down through other performers, stage directors and workshop leaders. To them we are indebted.

Where possible we have tried to acknowledge the source of a game we have adapted. In many cases, however, this has not been possible either because we have not been able to find a source or because there are a number of possible sources for a particular game.

Initially the exercises we adapted or created were designed to explore the more complex areas of singing and acting in performance. In trying to make these exercises work with all performers, irrespective of experience, we were encouraged to break them down into simpler component exercises. This led to our identifying the disciplines we thought fundamental to the process of singing and acting at the same time. The goal of a single unified expression relies first and foremost upon the practice of these disciplines.

Programmes of study in this area tend to focus on the triple areas of acting, singing and dancing. The importance of movement in this trinity cannot be overestimated, both as a skill in itself and as an essential part of characterisation. Whilst this book will involve many areas of physical action, it will not cover the area of dance and choreography per se. This lies outside our field of expertise. We hope that choreographers will not be insulted or disheartened by this omission. Nor will the book cover the specific area of how sound is produced or the techniques of voice production.

The exercises are designed to be used as one step in the development of your ideas. It is up to each individual to mix, adapt, develop and use the exercises to suit their own purposes. If used in this way our book will have contributed to the ongoing work of many who have made this field their life's quest.

Acknowledgements

We would like to thank the following publishers and authors for their kind permission to print the material included in this book: HarperCollins Publishers Ltd. (London) for permission to quote from Anthony Storr's *Music and the Mind*. Reprinted by permission of the Peter Fraser & Dunlop Group Ltd. W.W. Norton & Company (London) for permission to quote from Richard H. Hoppin's *Medieval Music*, and M. D. Herter Norton's translation of Rainer Maria Rilke's *Letters to a Young Poet*. The extract from *Sporting Body, Sporting Mind* by John Syer and Christopher Connolly is reproduced by kind permission of the publisher, Simon & Schuster Ltd. (London) © John Syer and Christopher Connolly 1984, 1987, 1998.

We would also like to express our warmest thanks to all those people who have read and commented on parts of the manuscript. In particular Fiona McAndrew and Ariane Gaborit whose patience and understanding have made this possible, Loic Nebreda, and Talia Rodgers. The final manuscript does not necessarily reflect their individually held opinions. Their comments have nevertheless proved invaluable. Thanks also to Gary Thorne for his illustration to *The Bird* and Jenny Arnold for her help with the physical warm-up.

We would also like to thank Andrew Alty, Peter Bailie, Jillian Barker, Neil Bartlett, Peter Berne, Charlotte Bishop, Nicolas Bloomfield, Ruth Burgess, Ali Campbell, Dominic Gray, Maria Jaugz, Michael Kennerley, Mary King, Beverley Klein, Jeffrey Lloyd Roberts, Lynne Plowman, Fiona Pinnell, Chrissie Poulter, Paul Reeve, Liz Rodger, Susan Sharpe, Rob Smith, Sheena Woolstencroft and the many other artists, friends and colleagues who have helped us come to a greater understanding of our work.

Part One   Introduction

1 Singing and acting in performance

INTRODUCTION

This book is about singing and acting at the same time. It is about playing. The playing of games and exercises to break down and reveal the world of singing and acting in performance. Games that unlock your individual potential as a performer while exploring those pragmatic questions common to all performers in sung theatre: How do I maintain the quality of acting whilst singing and the quality of singing whilst acting? How can I practise the integration of one with the other? What specific performance disciplines can I isolate and strengthen to achieve this integration?

From here more specific questions emerge: How can I use the written text and the score to create a coherent musical and dramatic interpretation? How can I find dramatic freedom within the formalised structure of music? How do the demands of the music affect my movement in a space? How do I incorporate the music into my construction of character? How can I explore rhythm and sound to create the inner life of my character? How do I cope with those anomalies of the genre that separate it from spoken theatre or the concert platform:

- Reacting spontaneously with other performers whilst remaining receptive to the energy of conductor and orchestra?
- Sustaining a physical and emotional impulse when time seems to accelerate, decelerate or even stop?
- Maintaining dramatic spontaneity when the text and music repeat over a period of time?
- Maintaining focus and intensity during fixed silences (musical rests) of varying lengths, or instrumental sections where there is no singing?

This list of questions, which is by no means exhaustive, has arisen from our practical work and discussion with performers and from the experiences of those we have worked with as stage director and musical director. We have conjured with many images in an attempt to capture the supreme act of mind and body co-ordination the performer undertakes when singing and acting at the same time. From the physical – spinning many plates in the air at the same time or rubbing several stomachs and patting several heads at once – to the spiritual – the uniting of opposites into a single act of truth. These images are a reflection of the many different ways performers perceive themselves and the craft they practise. Such metaphors can never fully reveal the magic or complexity of the art form. None the less they are born out of a desire to reveal and understand the special world that is created when music and drama unite.

This first chapter contains no games or exercises. It contains some of the observations and insights that have guided us in our search for ways in which to explore the art and form of sung theatre. Some of these conclusions may seem obvious, but they have none the less fuelled the invention of our exercises and, as such, provide a background to the chapters that follow. It has not been our intention to provide a definitive analysis of singing and acting. Whatever discussion takes place or whatever opinions are expressed, it is through the use of games and exercises that we hope to assert the right of each and every performer to discover their own answers to the questions above, whilst reaffirming the joy of playing both as the means and the end.

MUSIC AND DRAMA

At whatever level and in whatever way music and drama exist together in performance, when they do so, the expressive properties of one affect the other. The dramatic action, in which the events on stage unfold, and the text, which offers support and definition to the action, are transformed by the music which interprets, on its own terms, both action and text. For this reason when as a performer you change the way you sing the music, the drama will also change. Change the way you interpret your character and you alter the precise qualities of the music. This process may be conscious or unconscious. Similarly a change in tempo, whether faster or slower, or a change in the length of a pause may completely alter the flow of the dramatic scene and subsequently your performance. When you accept this then you have taken the first step to exploring and manipulating the music/drama mix.

The apparatus of musical expression revolves around the tensions created by combinations of rhythm, pitch, timbre (tone-colour) and volume and their arrangement into a texture. The apparatus of drama – essentially actions and words – differs in that neither time nor pitch are as fixed or formalised as they are in music. Music therefore provides the definition, or at least a skeleton, of time for drama. Drama on the other hand places music in the real world of story, situation, character and space.

The performer acts as the medium through which this relationship comes alive. In undertaking a transfer of personality whereby you behave as if you were somebody else, you make specific the musical world of the score and the dramatic actions suggested by the libretto or text. It is as if you are building a bridge between the reality of theatre, the representation of the human condition in all its beauty and imperfection, and the transcendental reality of music in all its perfection. This relationship between music and drama is a constantly shifting dynamic ranging from the presence of text and action without music to the presence of music without text or action. As spectators we may be tempted to separate the music and drama, for example commenting on a performer's singing or acting ability. In doing so we distance ourselves from the world of the performance. You may also be tempted to separate singing and acting in performance, concentrating on one rather than the other, but in doing so you will reduce your power to communicate total theatre and in particular you will risk losing a truthfulness of expression.

THE STRUCTURE OF SUNG THEATRE

The ways in which composers and librettists explore the relationship between music and drama present you with a series of challenges that occur as a result of the particular world of sung theatre. The structure of this world creates important opportunities for you in your role as communicator.

In sung theatre relative time and pitch are fixed. The fixed nature of musical time can dictate when you sing a word, when an action takes place or when an emotion is felt. It can construct the framework within which you initiate and complete an action or within which you reveal and resolve dramatic tensions. An inner understanding of the phenomenon of musical time will add strength and depth to your character's potential to express in a given situation. The benefits of this range from how you time stage business to how you sustain an emotion over extended periods of time. In performance, the performer in character is ideally perceived by the audience to be generating musical time rather than subject to it. In other words, your character is perceived to be creating or releasing the music. Without a control over the relationship between musical time and character, you are unlikely to take true creative ownership of your role. Moreover, finding a dramatic freedom within the formal structures of music will prove more elusive. When the processes of co-ordination necessary for this do not happen involuntarily at the moment of performance then the structure of music will conflict with the spontaneity of drama, acting as a block to truthfulness of character and emotion.

Musical pitches are arranged successively as melody and simultaneously as harmony. These are agents in your interpretation of the character's emotional journey. As pitch moves away from the register of normal speech the world of musical expression opens up and becomes an even greater part of the dramatic equation. This throws up many issues particularly with respect to the use of text. The inflection given to text in spoken drama is in itself a vehicle for expression. In sung theatre you are not normally free to choose whether your voice sounds at this or that pitch (i.e. the up and down of inflection). You therefore learn to make sense of and trust the composer's decisions in this respect. When you make these choices your own as part of your interpretation, you can reveal them in performance as if they are spontaneous expressions of your character and their emotion. In doing so you will find the power to unite the heightened emotional cry of sound and the concrete rational explanation of word.

In sung theatre our everyday notion of time passing is replaced by an architecture that seems to accelerate, decelerate or even suspend the moment. Music and drama illustrate a passage of events (in the widest sense) in different ways and subsequently set up and resolve their own tensions and conflicts differently. Viewed from both a dramatic and a musical perspective this causes difficulties with which performers, musical directors, stage directors, composers and librettists will need to come to terms in their work as a team. When music and drama interact, drama will inevitably provide a context for music. Music, however, does not necessarily need a context. Seen from one perspective drama can limit and oversimplify music's capacity to arouse an infinite number of emotional responses. Music, on the other hand, because it does not need to conform to an everyday notion of time in order to set up and resolve its own tensions, can make the passage of moments in drama seem false and even ridiculous.

However, as a direct result of the tensions that arise when music and drama engage with one another in theatre, a door appears through which we may be free to explore the complexity of a moment at many different levels of revelation. In other words you possess the power to create a new reality in which the worlds of the daily and the marvellous meet. A reality in which you are released to move between reason and feeling, the private and the public, the subconscious and the conscious. All this is made possible because the combination of music and drama allows you to simultaneously express contrasting thoughts and emotions. Any art may open a door to a new reality. In sung theatre, like other forms of theatre, you can reveal fresh perspectives on reality more forcefully by exploiting the specific form and structure of the medium in which you are working.

THE PAST, THE PRESENT AND THE CHALLENGE OF TERMINOLOGY

The origins of music as an art of the theatre are necessarily as obscure as the origins of music itself. As Anthony Storr points out in his fascinating book *Music and the Mind*:

> Making music appears to be one of the fundamental activities of mankind; as characteristically human as drawing and painting. The survival of Palaeolithic cave-paintings bears witness to the antiquity of this form of art; and some of these paintings depict people dancing. Flutes made of bone found in these caves suggest that they danced to some form of music. But, because music itself only survives when the invention of a system of notation has made a written record possible, or else

7

when a living member of a culture recreates the sounds
and rhythms which have been handed down to him by his
forebears, we have no information about prehistoric music.

(Storr 1993: 1)

The roots of music as an art of the theatre may well lie in
primitive ritual and ceremony. Sound and rhythm are both forces
within the process of ritualising. They alter our physical and
emotional state, they organise our actions, they allow common
experiences to be felt and shared. Furthermore dance and use of
the mask (to be found in early Palaeolithic engravings) remain
potent means of transcending our being and of representing other
planes of consciousness. This is true also of music and the fact that
musical sound is so much part of the fabric of human life suggests
that it played a greater part in the origins of theatre than can ever
be determined.

Whether the singing voice preceded the speaking voice or
vice versa is also a matter of debate. Some anthropologists have
speculated that vocal music began as a special way of communicating with the supernatural. In shamanistic rituals, the shaman
becomes a channel of communication with the other world and
reveals to the audience a mystical presence. Dance, incantation and
use of the mask in shamanistic practice require a skilfulness,
accomplishment and strength that go beyond the everyday. This
echoes the traditional notion that as a performer you are required
to develop a mastery of your craft and in particular the 'extra-daily'
physical and psychological power this demands. Indeed there is
a sense in which the act of meditation or chanting may be very
close to the set of mental and physiological conditions needed for
'engaged' performance.

In classical antiquity music and language are closely joined.
Once again, Anthony Storr in *Music and the Mind*:

There are a number of cultures which, like that of ancient
Greece, do not distinguish music as a separate activity from
those which it invariably accompanies. Singing, dancing, the
recitation of poetry, and religious chant are so inseparably
linked with music that there is no word for music as such.
Indeed, it may be difficult for the observer to determine
whether a particular activity includes music or does not.
Ceremonial speech may, as in the case of Greek poetry,

include rhythmic and melodic patterns which are so much part of it that words and music cannot really be differentiated.

(Storr 1993: 16–17)

In the late twentieth century the independence of music from words and movement is well established. Consequently we tend to think of music, drama and dance as separate arts. The history of sung theatre itself reveals a friction between words and music that the performer still encounters when doing justice to both librettist and composer or even stage director and musical director. The specialisation of music and spoken drama as separate art forms seems to have been part of the development already underway in ancient Greece. It was in the Middle Ages, however, that music was really to develop as a language with its own laws of structure and syntax. The intellectual pursuit of music as mathematical ratios related to sounds gave rise to a system of notation which could exist independently of the word. Inevitably, the polarity between word and music grew as music developed autonomously as an expressive form. From these developments to the present day the dynamic tension between word and music has fuelled innovation and debate. With reference to medieval music, Richard H. Hoppin states:

It is pertinent to note, first of all, that vocal music of any sort must reconcile two essentially irreconcilable demands: for straightforward and comprehensible presentation of the words, and for purely musical interest and attractiveness. One might write the entire history of vocal music in terms of the varied responses to these conflicting demands. Plain chant itself, despite its rather limited scope, illustrates the extremes that result from yielding to one demand or the other. In addition, we can observe an almost infinite gradation of inter-mediate compromises. The conflicting demands of text and music are responsible, at least in part, for the fundamental division of all plain chant into two stylistic categories: liturgical recitative and free composition.

(Hoppin 1978: 78)

In place of 'liturgical recitative' and 'free composition' in plain chant one could easily substitute the words 'recitative' and 'aria' in opera or 'verse' and 'refrain' in the musical.

Centuries later the voice was being explored as a musical instrument in itself. Composers and performers were preoccupied with pushing back the boundaries of vocal expression to create music that matched the pre-eminent expressive power of language. This was then placed within the context of theatre. Instead of simply organising music to fit the rhythmic pattern of poetic speech (recitative), composers wrote music which deviated from the rhythms of natural speech. These deviations were either contractions or expansions of natural speech patterns or ignored these patterns totally, exploiting the newfound capacity of music to organise words. This opened up space to express feeling in a structure where the narrative action of the story effectively stopped (aria). Many of the challenges you will encounter in singing and acting today result from the diverse ways in which artists have developed these initial experiments and exploited the balance and tension in the marriage of music and word, speech and sound. These represent two poles of our communication needs as human beings: the intuitive, instinctive world of abstract expression based on emotion and arousal which music explores so well, and the rational, analytical world of concrete expression based on definition that has become the preserve of the spoken word. The continuing existence of music as an art of the theatre in the form of operas and musicals is in part a reflection of our need to transcend this polarity, to experience total communication.

Given the history of sung theatre, it is not surprising that today every group with an interest in a production, from the singing teacher, stage director, musical director and choreographer to the company management, critic and spectator can encourage and indeed has encouraged the division between 'singer' and 'actor'. This may spring from pragmatic considerations when casting or assessing a production. However, where this division exists in your own mind, you risk limiting yourself even if you feel you are playing to your strengths. The pressure to separate singing and acting is almost irresistible. Consider how you learn a role. When you commit a role to memory you will perform many operations in a purely technical capacity, such as learning the notes so that they are well placed vocally or making vocal adjustments based on the requirements of the role. By and large you will begin this work without knowing what the stage director and musical director have in mind for the overall production. Yet the longer you continue technical work in isolation without a dramatic conception, the greater the risk that technical accomplishment becomes an end in itself. When you finally start production rehearsals, singing and acting may already have become two separate functions.

The division between 'singer' and 'actor' may also be due in part to the training for performers of sung theatre. What this does not provide, irrespective of whether this is undertaken in a drama college or music college, is a training in general musicianship (for example, the exploration of how pitches and rhythm combine and relate) that takes place within a theatrical context (for example, the exploration of situation, character and space). Although there are some notable exceptions, colleges tend to teach the constituent parts – singing, acting, movement – but offer little if any provision for their integrated study. This encourages performers to see the expressive possibilities of each element only in relation to itself. An approach that explores the expressive possibilities that lie in the interrelationship of music, drama and movement should constitute part of the performer's training. This would take account of the very real differences that exist for you as a performer of sung theatre. These differences are themselves seldom acknowledged, resulting in an acting training that has more to do with the demands of spoken theatre and a musical training that has more to do with the demands of the concert platform.

This situation further reinforces many performers' perception of themselves as either 'actors' or 'singers' depending upon the emphasis and value that has been placed on either singing or acting within a course of study. The net result is that the task of integration is left to the performer in rehearsal when preparing for a production. The particular pressures that accompany production rehearsals do not and should not allow for a detailed practised study of how music and drama combine and interrelate, as this itself requires among other things repetition, reflection and assimilation. Without this study however you are effectively learning to cling to a limited range of techniques which you hope will see you through. In effect the rehearsal relies upon making use of what you already bring hidden in your 'bag of tools'. This book will encourage the development and sharpening of your resources so that you are freer in mind, body and voice to explore the entirety of music and drama in the rehearsal and performance of sung theatre.

The term 'sung theatre' is our response to the absence of a generic term which embraces the entire art and activity of the theatre in Western culture in which performers both sing and act simultaneously. In other words opera, operetta, musical theatre, vaudeville, cabaret and music theatre. That opera and the musical do have separate names may reflect their status in a culture. However, it is futile to draw boundaries between them in purely formalistic terms. It is also difficult to articulate these boundaries without imposing or at least implying a value judgement. Certainly, the forms of opera and the musical demand that we make different choices regarding the musical aesthetic and these affect decisions as to what kind of performer will best fulfil the vocal requirements of a role. Decisions relating to the musical aesthetic will affect what is demanded of you in rehearsal. Describing the technical requirements of a particular style is an area that will not be covered by this book. We are concerned here with the wider issue – that both opera and the musical demand an integration of music and drama. This question has not only preoccupied composers throughout history but has also become a benchmark by which their work is understood today. From Monteverdi, Gluck and Mozart through to Gershwin, Rogers and Hart, Rogers and Hammerstein, Bernstein and Sondheim, the only unbroken tradition has been a conscious commitment to unite music and drama.

There are a number of possible expressions that could be used as a means of referring to this theatre. Of these the term 'music theatre' has the most currency, but is full of ambiguities. It was adopted in English from the German *Musiktheater* and since the late 1940s the term has acquired more and more semantic baggage. It carries firstly the notion of renewing the operatic tradition as used originally by Walter Felsenstein, founder of the Komische Oper in Berlin, to reflect his work on the inter-dependency of music and stage action. Since then it has continued to suggest a renewal of interpretation in opera, particularly by companies performing operatic repertoire who nevertheless wish to distance themselves from many of the associations which the word 'opera' brings with it. It is also used to label the creation of new work (not necessarily contemporary opera) including interdisciplinary and experimental work.

The alternatives to 'music theatre' are no less fraught. The term 'music drama' is somewhat literary and is also associated specifically with the theories and practice of Richard Wagner. Like 'theatre', which can refer to an activity, a repertoire or a building, the word 'drama' may refer to performance or literature. The 'lyric theatre' sounds too lofty, and 'musicodramatic entertainment' too academic. There is a sense in which practitioners and public alike are comfortable with the language of traditional categories (opera, operetta, musical, etc.), until, that is, they must refer to a piece of performance repertoire that does not fit so obviously or neatly into any one category, such as works by Weill, Bernstein, Adams or even Sondheim. However, for the purposes of our book we need a term of ready reference and in using 'sung theatre' we accept that this may not find a currency outside of this book.

In omitting reference to non-Western theatre we do not wish to imply that music as an art of the theatre is somehow the sole preserve of Western culture. Clearly it is not as is demonstrated by the close association of music with theatre which is to be found in the many different cultures across the world today. For example, in Japan where the form of theatre known as Kabuki (literally 'ka' song, 'bu' dance, 'ki' art, skill) uses music to indicate place, time and mood. Rather Western theatre, and in particular opera and the musical, happens to be our area of concern and experience as practitioners. It is from the absence of a codified system of rules for performance in Western theatre that the need for practical work such as our own arises in the first place.

THE PERFORMER

As a performer you have a direct responsibility for the relationship between your character's music, text and movement at any moment of performance. You have a shared responsibility for the relationship with other elements. For example, other characters and their music, text and movement, the orchestra and conductor and the external elements of design. Therefore the choices you make will directly affect the relationship other performers are creating between music, text and movement. By the same token, choices that other performers make will, of course, affect the relationship between your music, text and movement. Each one of these elements is expressive both in relation to itself and in relation to other elements. For this reason the choice for expression in performance (in terms of what you want to reveal) is both vast and exciting. In addition the technical requirements demanded of you are equally vast and exciting. They range from the athleticism needed to sustain physical and vocal energy over an extended period of time to the imagination needed to find a means of expression that remains truthful however near or far the structure of time moves from the everyday.

A frequent criticism of sung theatre, especially from the viewpoint of spoken theatre, is that the works and productions are 'superficial'. Beyond the question of individual taste implied here, such criticism may have a point. A work and/or a production may appear superficial where those involved, from stage director and music director through to composer and writer, have not taken responsibility for the interrelationship of the expressive elements. The journey from audition to first night is complex not least because there are so many individuals involved in the creative process leading to performance. The many relationships that create expression in sung theatre exist whether or not the individuals involved in a production recognise and respond to them. The music will *always* affect the drama. Therefore it seems sensible to make musical choices that support dramatic choices rather than undermine them. On the one hand a failure to recognise this can lead to a lack of coherence caused by the individual elements being expressive in themselves but not in relation to the other elements – in other words different elements pull in different directions. On the other hand it may produce a one-dimensional theatre where the different elements are effectively communicating as if on the same frequency. In other words there is no tension established between them which results in over simplified emotions and generalised acting.

Whatever takes place during rehearsal, it is the performer who appears on stage before an audience and it is the performer who should be given ultimate responsibility for interpretation. You hold your character's music and drama within a balance of your making.

THE FUNDAMENTAL DISCIPLINES

Managing this task of co-ordination effectively depends on your ability to embody the following disciplines:

1 RELAXATION To develop and maintain the ability to eliminate tensions of all kinds from your body and mind. In removing obstacles to the free flow of energy you become

prepared – physically, mentally, emotionally – to act with focus and clarity. A relaxed concentration is also a prerequisite to vocal production. This is a state of active stillness.

2 FITNESS, FLEXIBILITY AND CONTROL To develop and maintain your physical, vocal and mental fitness, flexibility and control. This also builds upon work at the most fundamental level of music – flexibility and control of the dynamics of pitch, timbre and volume. This is a state of agility and alertness.

3 CONCENTRATION To develop and maintain your ability to concentrate instantaneously with unusual power, attending fully to the necessary and eliminating the unnecessary. This state is allied to relaxation.

4 AWARENESS To develop and maintain an openness to interact with others including other performers as characters and the audience. In sung theatre this also involves a conductor and orchestra. This relies upon your internal and external awareness.

5 IMAGINATION AND SPONTANEITY To develop and maintain the ability of your imagination to help you manifest yourself physically, vocally and mentally. This is a state (to use Eugenio Barba's phrase) of the 'dilated mind' or 'dilated body'. Furthermore to develop a spontaneity which allows you to respond to what actually happens as opposed to what you expect to happen.

These disciplines are central to the preparation and execution of any co-ordinated activity. In addition to these the act of interpretation in sung theatre requires specific attention to the following areas:

1 VOICE PRODUCTION The ability to obtain from your voice any kind of tone, of any quality and duration at any speed of succession in response to the demands of the score and your interpretation of a character in a given situation.

2 RHYTHM AND PULSE a) Pulse: The ability to inwardly feel the musical pulse, thereby avoiding any external manifestation of this, so that your body is free to undertake the external activities demanded by your interpretation of a character in a given situation. The ability to feel the pulse inwardly engages your sense of time at the seat of the emotions. b) Rhythm: The

15

ability to divide and then subdivide the beat accurately and automatically so that rhythmic patterns are merely part of the forward movement of the pulse, so that your mind and body are free to create and react.

3 DICTION AND APPRECIATION OF WORDS The ability to deliver the vowels and consonants that make up words with a sufficient clarity and intensity in order to engage with the emotions demanded by your interpretation of a character in a given situation.

4 CHARACTERISATION The ability to harness the circumstances provided by text, music and production in order to create and portray a character. Allied to this is the ability to project and sustain the emotions of this character in response to your inner life as a performer and elements external to you, such as the musical accompaniment and other characters in a given situation.

THE INDIVISIBLE EXPRESSION

As a practitioner your organisational task is to combine these areas into a single co-ordinated act of sung theatre. It is possible to transcend the separate performance disciplines involved in singing and acting at the same time to unite the many levels of meaning present in music and drama into a synthesis. This synthesis appears to the spectator in one moment of time as one indivisible expression. We can think of this indivisible expression as a living harmony whereby the independent elements that make up music and drama are voluntarily united into a single organism, engaged and alive at every moment of performance. This act occurs through the way in which you allow elements such as rhythm, pitch, gesture, action, words and space to express independently of one another and more particularly in the way in which you allow them to express in their relationship to one another. In order to do this as an artist you will use those characteristics that make you unique – in particular your personality, sensibility and the particular imprint of your voice.

USING THE EXERCISES

The overall idea behind the exercises is to bring the needs of drama and of music into creative interplay with one another. By emphasising your personal creativity and the choices you can and must make, the exercises will lead you towards a more total performance where those choices are integrated with the demands of score and situation. Initially we have tried to identify the fundamental skills required to co-ordinate and have written exercises designed to strengthen the precision, power and flexibility of these skills in preparation for the more complex exercises. These more complex exercises offer ways in which you can perceive, unlock and practise the full potential of both music and drama in a work. In doing so your responsiveness to the creative input of stage director and musical director is increased. These exercises will therefore develop your power to communicate sung theatre.[1]

These exercises are appropriate for any performer from the beginner to the professional. You can use many of the exercises on your own as preparation for workshop, rehearsal or performance. A large proportion of the exercises are applicable to a group session. It is of course vital that you practise on your own and acquire as many skills as possible. However, it is when you work with other people that the greatest provocation and response occurs.[2]

Some of these exercises are deliberately simple. We feel that developing a highly focused and detailed application to the simplest tasks is essential to understanding and embracing the most difficult challenges. Many of the exercises in this book are based on games. These can be useful as such, played for their own sake so that through the enjoyment of the game there naturally follows a release of energy and tension. Any game can become an exercise through an awareness of areas of skill and technical disciplines contained within it. Maintaining a game at a simple level will not sustain energy and interest for long. Focusing on specific disciplines moves the playing on to a higher level whereby you use the game to confront your limits. This can then be applied to the demanding nature of your performance work.[3] Notes in the margin highlight areas of technique and contain additional information for anyone leading a group exercise. All the games and exercises have arisen from challenges faced in rehearsals and we have where necessary related an exercise to its application

1 For the stage director and musical director (teacher, workshop leader) the exercises and the ideas behind them will clarify the opportunities and challenges inherent in performing sung theatre, increasing your capacity to facilitate the performer.

2 The exercises will produce different results when placed in a different order within an overall workshop plan. A group will be stimulated not only by exploring the exercise itself but also by the passage from one exercise to the next.

3 Once again a game may be played for enjoyment alone, especially when technical considerations begin to inhibit the performer. It may be necessary with some games to introduce the elements of technical discipline gradually.

17

4 Each exercise is given a title and an indication of the particular skills being practised. We suggest a time span for each exercise, both for planning and as an indication of the level of application needed. This is a rough guide only and assumes a certain level of co-operation. Less disciplined or less confident groups may require more time.

Resources are listed at the beginning of each exercise. Invariably you will need to make some calculations relating to group size.

Risk relates to the level at which the exercise exposes the individual. High risk might involve improvised solo singing in front of the group; medium risk a degree of individual singing, not necessarily improvised; low-risk activities shelter the individual within the group dynamic. Dramatically speaking, the activities might involve greater or lesser degrees of trust. These categories are merely a guide and relate above all to a workshop situation with less experienced group members.

5 It is counter-productive for the performer to think too much about the

in rehearsal and performance. Overall you may return to many of the games/exercises in this book at different stages of your development and make different use of them.[4]

THE WORKSHOP PROCESS

Many of the ideas in this book can be explored through the work-shop process, where it is hoped that you will be given the time and space to apply ideas and techniques unhindered by the particular pressures that accompany rehearsals.[5] The workshop process is a means by which you can explore, discover and assimilate. This will inevitably involve the removing of obstacles, the isolating and exercising of skills and a process of re-assembling them into a more complete whole. If this process is to work then you must be pre-pared to be honest about who you are. Put another way, as an artist you are always concerned with communicating an understanding and a feeling. There is a point where it becomes impossible to dissociate this from personal revelation.

The workshop process will inevitably challenge and sometimes force you to ask questions in relation to how and why you have chosen to perform. The following questions are worth reflection. You may like to consider them (at any stage of your career) as a way to prepare for the honesty and determination to search that performance demands.

1 Do you really love what you do? Why? When was the last time you asked yourself this question?

2 Are you always motivated to work? Are you prepared to forgive yourself when you're not?

3 Are you happy with the way you practise? For example, do you pay sufficient attention to detail? Do you pay too much attention to detail and lose sight of a wider picture?

4 Do you allow yourself enough time to prepare for rehearsal? For example, to learn the score and maintain independent training in different performance areas to ensure that you are in optimum condition for every rehearsal and performance? What aspects of your preparation for rehearsal receive the most and least attention?

5 Do you balance the enjoyment of what you can do with the improvement of what you cannot? Do you place too much

pressure on yourself to overcome technical difficulties too quickly?

6 Do you balance the need to persevere with the need to take a break, change your activity or rest? Do you take time to enjoy and celebrate your talents irrespective of the need to improve?

7 Do you trust that many improvements do not happen at the moment of rehearsal or individual study but are assimilated in between, often during moments of rest?

8 Do you feel that your background research (for example, in the field of music, theatre practice, literature, drama, art, society or politics) equips you adequately to interpret a role?

9 Are you able to take risks in rehearsal? Do you allow yourself the right to try things out without fear of failure? Are there any particular circumstances that may influence this? Do you encourage your fellow performers to try things out without fear of failure? Do you feel that you are open and responsive to the creative risks taken by your fellow performers?

10 Do you balance an openness to listen and respond to the ideas and energy of others with a willingness to express constructively your own ideas and opinions both in rehearsal and performance?

11 Do you feel confident enough to take criticism? How much positive encouragement do you need to move forward? Are you able to give positive encouragement to others? Are you too self-critical? Do you encourage too much criticism from others?

12 What aspects of your musical and dramatic ability would you like to improve? Do these coincide with the comments of stage directors, musical directors and other sources of feedback?

13 In what way is your vocal technique separate from or integrated into the other demands that are made of you on stage or indeed your development and growth as a person?

purpose behind an exercise before doing it. It is better to discover this through participating in the exercise. Too much prior discussion can put pressure on the performer to achieve an end result – a pressure all too familiar in rehearsal. Conversely, it is important to discuss the performer's state of awareness after an exercise. If necessary repeat an exercise several times until members of the group have taken the process on board both mentally and physically. Problems and blocks may not be solved immediately but the performer must be aware of them so that while away from the exploratory environment the unconscious will continue to work on a solution.

THE LEADER AND THE WORKSHOP PROCESS

From a leader's point of view a workshop involves three major processes. Firstly, that of *inclusion*. Icebreakers are generally used to begin a workshop and for good reason. You will ask the group in the workshop to go beyond what they believe their limitations to be. With this in mind it is vital to create a safe environment and to choose exercises which are appropriate to the group's needs. Real learning takes place best in a joyous and non-judgemental environment. Here a workshop leader needs to think about the mental attitude of the group as well as their feelings and physical needs. Exercises which are too challenging will not create a safe environment, while exercises which are not challenging enough will lower expectations and make the more challenging work which comes later less possible. As always, thorough planning and the ability to abandon the plan itself if needs be (particularly when working with a group whose needs are unfamiliar to you) are vital elements of a successful workshop. Background research into the needs of the group is an invaluable asset at this stage.

A leader also needs to have an awareness of how to handle problems encountered during the inclusion process, in particular late arrivals and personalities who need to be seen and heard to the detriment of co-operative work. Many of the problems that arise require you to balance the needs of the individual with the needs of the group. It is difficult to prescribe ways of dealing with these problems other than to say that they must be recognised and resolved at an early stage before moving on to more difficult work. You will need to reinforce the process of inclusion throughout the workshop period and particularly after a long break (for example, after lunch).

The second process for a leader to think about is that of *assertion*. Much of the workshop will involve the leader giving instructions. These need to be clear and precise but it is also important that the group listens to the instructions and carries them out as indicated, not as an approximation to what was indicated. You may need to build certain exercises into the workshop at an early stage to facilitate this process. For example, instruction games. Negotiate this stage successfully and you will create within the group a confidence to express personal ideas. Further to this, it is worth noting that instructions often contain implicit judgements that imply the possibility of success or failure. At all times a leader should beware of using language that is value laden and of asking questions that in fact answer themselves.

This in turn leads to the final process, sometimes referred to as '*the death of the leader*', whereby the group challenges the work and eventually takes control to ensure that its needs are met. A leader who tries to maintain too much control at this stage will limit the work unnecessarily since they will not be open to the many possibilities the group has to offer. The workshop process will also flounder in that the benefit of the exercises will rely upon the presence of a leader for affirmation who sooner or later will not be there. The most important thing is that the performer can take away the skills explored and developed within a workshop and use them when working with other leaders in rehearsal or devising work. The precise stage at which you hand over to the group will depend largely on that group's development. Ultimately (possibly after a number of sessions) it should be possible for the group to develop the next stage of the workshop for themselves. Having understood the different stages constructed by the leader they should be in a position to direct the next stage.

This final point also relates to the way in which you choose to construct the learning process in workshops. All too often rehearsals involve a monologic method whereby instructions are given that the performer then undertakes. Often this method is necessary. If someone is singing a wrong note then it is usually enough to point this out as a matter of fact which the performer is required then to sort out either on their own or with the help of a pianist, musical director or coach. But in other areas of work the dialogic approach is far more effective, whereby you facilitate through question, dialogue and confirmation to focus the performer and to draw knowledge from within them. As the workshop proceeds it is vital to engage this more active learning process – a joint learning inquiry where everyone has a contribution to make – since it will increase the responsiveness of participants and facilitate them to work in a much more creative way.

There are many possible components to the workshop process. At different times it may seem sensible to include some and omit others. However, these are some suggestions for you to think about:

1 Demand and facilitate a high level of commitment from participants through a process of observation and encouragement.
2 Ensure that there is sufficient physical activity at different stages of the workshop combining the physical and the mental at different points and relating the two wherever possible.
3 Ensure that you share the enthusiasm of the group.
4 Ensure that there are sufficient breaks and that these are positioned strategically to make the most of the workshop day

in terms of the participants' concentration levels and the logical passage of exercises from theme to theme.

5 Ensure that at times you participate in the exercises. In other words find a balance between leading from outside and leading from within.

6 Ensure that you explain the aims and objectives of the workshop to the group and that the workshop itself meets the expectations of the participants. In this respect thorough planning and good time management should leave space for the group to feed back at regular intervals. Being aware of the needs of a group does not necessarily demand a change of activity but it will certainly affect the language you use and the approach you take towards an exercise.

7 Ensure that the achievement targets are clear within your mind when planning and leading the workshop.

8 Ensure that there is a transfer of power to the group during the session, which facilitates the progress of individual responsibility.

9 Ensure that members of the group learn through both participation and observation. At times observing the experiences of others can facilitate the development of a group member's own activities. A group member may find it easier to apply knowledge gained from observation.

10 Ensure that any ground rules are clearly explained and enforced if necessary for the benefit of the whole group.

11 Provide for the possibility of risk-taking in a safe environment through encouragement and protection of the less confident members of the group.

12 Ensure that the workshop is structured in such a way that through the logical organisation of exercises the learning areas will be made intuitively evident to the group.

13 Ensure that there is a good general level of audibility both within the group and particularly on your part.

14 Ensure that there is a mechanism for complaints or the venting of frustrations especially concerning yourself.

While the goals of a workshop may be clear and the benefits ultimately directed towards the individual, it is important to remember that the mechanism for this is a group activity. The workshop form involves individuals working closely together which means that as a leader you must constantly monitor the feelings of individuals towards each other and build cohesion within the group as a necessary mechanism for individual development. This alongside the monitoring of the way in which individuals develop during the course of the workshop.

Part Two The Exercises

2 The fundamental disciplines

PREPARING THE GROUND

In sung theatre the challenge of singing and acting simultaneously begins at the simplest level of activity. Here you must prepare the ground for the complex tasks of co-ordination that lie ahead. To give an idea of the challenge you face, try the following experiment. With your right hand trace a circle in the air. Then with your left hand trace a square. Now do both at the same time without loss of accuracy or fluidity.

Faced with the task of integrating singing and acting into one means of expression, you need to co-ordinate the many different elements of expression at your disposal without loss of focus or clarity. When negotiating a complicated vocal line, your characterisation of movement may dissipate. For example, gestures may become vague or lack motivation. When negotiating a complicated action on stage you may forget your words or lose the musical pulse. You may find yourself out of time with the orchestra or not really listening to the other characters on stage. In other words one activity may lead to a loss of control and clarity in another. The act of singing itself requires great co-ordination. This is not to say that we should be in awe of it. It is no less or more fantastic and complex than breathing and like breathing much of the process is an unconscious one. It is just that as practitioners we study parts of this process *explicitly*, picking apart the mechanism of the voice and reassembling it. This brings with it a *technical* awareness of what it is to sing which must nevertheless support and not stifle the *natural* feeling of what it is to sing. The preparation in this chapter embraces fundamental disciplines, such as relaxation, concentration and awareness. It practises simple acts of co-ordination and also introduces the technique of *dissociation*.   **27**

The exercises in this chapter are not technically complicated. Their simplicity should allow you to:

- Focus on the act of co-ordinating different activities.
- Give space to the imagination unfettered by excessive technical requirements.
- Allow for detailed observation as to how one activity is affected by the simultaneous execution of another.
- Build up an awareness of how a physical activity will affect a vocal activity and vice versa.[1]

RELAXATION

Controlling your physical and mental resources is dependent first and foremost upon your ability to relax. This ability would seem to be innate but you should be able to access this state at will. Amongst many symptoms, tension may distort the voice and impair rhythmic ability. If you are tense you think less positively and less efficiently. Commands are not transmitted with fluidity and precision, sensation is suffocated and expression restrained. In other words, tension prevents you from making full use of your physical, mental and emotional energy.

Furthermore, the audience naturally imitates internally the rhythm and shape of your performance. This is an important part of their contact. Any tension will transmit itself to an audience and in so doing will decrease its sense of pleasure in the participation of the drama.

Removing blocks in the body caused by tension is an ongoing process. Many tensions are habitual, unconsciously nurtured over the years. These are often linked to the work you do and how you feel or have felt about it. In a way tension marks your physical and mental history, whether long term as a result of life experiences or short term in the specific lead up that day, week or hour to the moment of rehearsal or performance. Trauma and history may become locked into the body as tension. Your mind and body must learn to recognise this history before discarding it. This process of recognition is a very personal one as it deals with your own self awareness. In the long term it is more productive to look at the cause of tension, as removing the symptoms may only serve to place the tension elsewhere in the body where it will later

1 Practise and develop these exercises regularly. Remember that a different ordering of exercises will produce different results. We have chosen not to include the numerous group warm-up and 'ice-breaker' games we often use in practice, as these are covered extensively in other works (see bibliography).

resurface. Physical tension rebuilds very quickly even after a solid and productive warm-up.

In the mind, tension leads to anxiety and vice versa. The nature of the performer's work means that you are affected by varying degrees of anxiety. This is quite different, though at times difficult to distinguish, from excitement. There is, however, a point where anxiety will affect the performance.

Relaxation clears the unhelpful stresses that have been stored away before the performance begins. This frees you of blocks or interferences that may inhibit your ability to communicate or respond. This includes attitudes such as fear of failure and self-doubt that often manifest themselves through a self-critical 'inner voice'. Many performers find that a particular technique (such as Yoga, Alexander Technique, Tai Chi, meditation or positive affirmations) practised over a long period can help with this. Relaxation also figures in the process of warming down after a period of intense work.

Relaxation is not static. The aim of relaxation is either to withdraw completely to allow for the regeneration of energy or withdraw temporarily to reduce tension to a productive level. Think of relaxation as an alert stillness or a still alertness.

Paradoxically one gains control by giving up the need to control. The object is always to let the performance happen rather than to make it happen.

EXERCISE 1

Title: The Inventory

Destination: Corporeal awareness

Via: Progressive muscular relaxation

Time Needed: 30+ minutes

Risk: Low

Resources: A mat, a quiet warm space

Instructions[2]

a.   Lie down on your back (knees raised so that the soles of your feet are in contact with the floor) and put your arms by your sides. Allow yourself to feel comfortable.

2 This exercise makes use of *kinesthesis* – your internal awareness of the position and movement of the muscles of your body. It forms the basis of the singer's autonomic co-ordination when singing and is the sense that enables us to read the impulses and intentions of others. The more you become aware of this sense the greater the flexibility you will have to change and respond. The exercise also encourages a conscious release of tension from the body.   **29**

b. Close your eyes and allow your mouth to open slightly by relaxing your jaw . . . As you breathe in and out (through the mouth), allow your breath to find its own natural rhythm . . . Follow the stream of your breath as you breathe in deeply . . . and out . . . As you breathe in, feel your breath filling your body . . . As you breathe out, allow all distractions to drift away . . . In . . . and out . . . Repeat this several times.

c. Now pay attention to your feet . . . become aware of them and explore how they feel . . . Can you distinguish the different toes from each other? . . . Can you differentiate the ball of your foot from the heel? . . . Do this for both feet . . . Can you feel a difference between your right and left foot? . . . Slowly tighten the muscles in your feet . . . sustain . . . and let go . . . Allow your feet to feel heavy and warm . . .

d. Now focus on your calves and knees . . . Become aware of the area surrounding your ankle and sense the muscles that connect to your calves until your reach the back of your knee . . . Feel a line of energy between your knees and ankles . . . Slowly tighten the muscles from your knees to your ankles . . . sustain . . . and let go . . . Feel the tension dissipate . . .

e. Now become aware of each of your thighs. Sense the weight of each thigh . . . sense the volume of your thighs . . . Allow them to become loose and heavy . . . Think your way around from the backs of your thighs to the front and back again . . . Feel a line of energy between your knees and your thigh muscles . . . Slowly tighten the thigh muscles . . . sustain . . . and let go . . .

f. Now find a path from the muscles of your thighs to those of your buttocks . . . Find a path from the muscles of your buttocks to those of your groin . . . Sense the weight of the muscles in the buttocks and groin . . . Sense their volume . . . How many different paths can you find emanating from the muscles in this area to the rest of the body? . . . Slowly tighten the muscles in your buttocks, groin and pelvis . . . sustain . . . and let go . . .

g. Allow your breath to flow in . . . and out . . . and relax . . . Shift your attention now to the abdomen . . . Feel the muscles of your abdomen . . . Concentrate on these muscles and feel how they move as you breathe . . . Slowly tighten the muscles in your abdomen . . . and sustain . . . and let go . . .

h. Now focus on your chest and rib cage . . . Breathe in and release any tension in your chest as you breathe slowly out . . . and in again . . . Feel how your chest and abdomen expand and contract as you breathe . . .

i. Now become aware of your shoulders . . . If possible allow them both to sink into the ground . . . Where are your shoulder blades? . . . Discover the way in which they are connected to the arms . . . Think of the weight of the muscles in your shoulders . . . sense their volume . . . allow them to become loose and heavy . . . eventually you feel them becoming warmer . . . Tense the muscles in your shoulders . . . sustain . . . and let go . . .

j. Now focus on each section of your arms . . . become aware of your upper arms and the way in which they are connected to your shoulders at one end and your elbows at the other . . . become aware of the connection between your elbows and your wrists . . . and finally pay attention to your hands . . . Explore each hand finger by finger then joint by joint . . . Think of the bones in each of your fingers . . . think of the muscles surrounding them . . . the nails . . . the skin . . . Tense the muscles in your arms and hands . . . sustain . . . and let go . . .

k. Now become aware of your neck . . . Find the different pathways of muscles that connect your head to the rest of your body . . . Spend some time with the front of your neck . . . Spend some time with the back of your neck . . . Tense the muscles in your neck . . . sustain . . . and let go . . . Allow these muscles to become loose and heavy . . .

l. Now focus on the whole of your back . . . Move up and down the length of your spine . . . Can you feel it in contact with the floor? . . . Think of the muscles surrounding each and every one of your vertebrae . . .

m. Now bring your attention back to the front of your neck . . . and move on to your face . . . Explore your forehead and the muscles around your eyes . . . and your jaw muscles . . . think of the weight of these muscles . . . allow them to become loose and heavy . . . become aware of the different pathways between your jaws and your chin, lips, cheeks, nose and ears . . . Now bring your attention to your teeth, tongue and other features inside your mouth . . . How does the inside of your mouth feel different to the outside of your face? . . . Tense the muscles in your forehead . . . and around your eyes . . . and in your jaw . . . and your whole face . . . and sustain . . . and let go . . .

n. Breathe in . . . and out . . . and relax . . . Now investigate your whole body beginning with your forehead and moving over the top of your head down the length of your spine through your buttocks, the backs of your legs to the ankles and soles of your feet and then moving through your toes and the front of your feet up through the top of the body until you reach your forehead once more . . . Become aware of your body as the sum of all these parts working together . . .

o. As you do so you feel calm and relaxed . . . Be aware of this feeling and know that whenever you feel tense, you can return to a relaxed state by reflecting on this internal photograph you have taken . . .

p. Now slowly return your attention to the room . . . begin to move your body . . . and open your eyes.

There are many different ways of exploring this exercise. Using different routes to explore the map of the body may engender different sensations and produce different results. Another method is to use a visualisation technique. For example, you imagine yourself on a beach and that the sun is warming each individual part of your body which is then cooled by a gentle breeze. Alternatively think of a golden light or the energy of the earth coming up from the ground under your feet and flowing through your body to connect all its progressively relaxed parts.

DISSOCIATION

Simply stated, this technique is the ability to co-ordinate two or more areas of focus whilst maintaining an independent control over each one. Using the metaphor of the square and the circle, this would mean being able to do the two activities at the same time but also to change the dynamic of either one independently of the other. For example, accelerating the speed of the circle while maintaining the speed of the square. In this chapter these co-ordination skills are introduced at a manageable level. This marks the beginning of your exploration of relationships between action, word and music.

It is natural to associate the articulation of gesture, word and music within a similar dynamic. For example, strong music often provokes a direct gesture. Whilst there may be a good dramatic reason for this – angry people may indeed shake their fists, raise their voices and spit their words – it may not always, if ever, reveal enough about the character in a given situation. When exploring interpretation, the technique of dissociation can equip you with the means to create more powerful associations between movement, sound and word. For example, strong music accompanied by a less direct gesture may reveal an angry character ill at ease with this emotion. The technique of dissociation may require you to consciously act against a 'natural' tendency to restate the emotion in the music with your gesture and diction. As a performer you are, like any human being, subject to the power that music has to change our physiological and psychological (in particular emotional) state. However, you must be able to separate the emotional response you have to the music from the demands of your character in situation.

Dissociating the dynamic energies of music, gesture and word is an essential part of your craft in sung theatre. An independent control of gesture, word and music, and all their constituent parts, will free you to exploit the potential of contrasts and opposites. Work based on an awareness of opposites, as in the example above, will tap a richer seam of meaning and ultimately a more profound expression of character. Independent parts come together as one energy within you and a synthesis occurs that contains the spirit of contrasts. This synthesis allows you to open the spectator's perception in unexpected ways.

EXERCISE 2

Title: Exchange
Destination: Corporeal awareness
Via: Muscular co-ordination and isolation
Time Needed: 15 minutes at a time
Risk: Low
Resources: A mat, a quiet warm place

Instructions[3]

a. Lie down on your back with the soles of your feet on the floor and your knees raised. Close your eyes and allow your breathing to settle. You should feel comfortable and relaxed.

b. Tense the muscles in your right arm and sustain the tension for several seconds before releasing. Repeat this making sure that any tension is fully released.

c. Repeat this same process with your left arm.

d. Next repeat the same process alternating between each arm. Leave ten seconds between the relaxation of one arm and the tensing of the other.

[3] In order to 'dissociate', you need first to 'isolate'. This exercise looks at contracting one muscle group while relaxing another. It is designed as a first step in instructing the body and mind to dissociate. Exercise 1 is a useful preparation for this exercise.

33

e.   Gradually reduce the time between the relaxation of one arm and the tensing of the other until they follow on from one another fluidly (without pause).

f.   Next repeat the process described above, alternating between different parts of the body. For example: right leg/left leg, right leg/left arm, left hand/left upper arm, right foot/left foot.[4]

VISUALISATION

Visualisation is a useful technique for both relaxation and imagination. It relies upon the natural power of the imagination to create strong mental pictures. You may 'guide' these images to a greater or lesser extent. Either allow impressions to act upon the mind or actively choose and create what you wish to see or imagine. Both types of visualising are important. Some people see very clear pictures when they close their eyes and imagine something. Other people do not form mental pictures as such but become aware of a heightened feeling. An adaptation may be necessary that places more emphasis on the other senses (touch, smell, taste, sound). Many people will find the technique of visualisation difficult, especially at the beginning. If this is the case then work on your concentration and imagination first.

You can use the technique of visualisation on your own or as a group. If you are by yourself, try recording a voice speaking the text to guide the visualisation. After a period of time, as the exercise becomes second nature, the tape may no longer be necessary. Record your tape in a quiet place and read slowly with appropriate pauses at the ellipsis points (. . .) and at the end of paragraphs.

EXERCISE 3

Title: Changing Places

Destination: To release the body and mind from anxiety and reduce tension

Via: Visualisation

Time Needed: 15+ minutes

Risk: Low

Resources: A chair, a quiet warm place

4 Placing a tension in one specific area of the body often leads automatically to a tension forming elsewhere. Isolate only the specific tension required. Repetition will build up your power to isolate the smallest muscle groups. As the time between relaxing and tensing decreases, you may hold a residual tension in a part of the body. This is because the act of tensing one part of the body can impede the relaxation of another. If this happens, stop the exercise and re-establish a relaxed state before continuing.

Instructions[5]

a. Find a place where you can sit undisturbed for fifteen to twenty minutes. Close your eyes, become aware of your breathing and if necessary allow its rhythm to settle by taking and releasing long deep breaths. As you do so allow your body to relax from the head downwards. With each exhalation you feel your body sinking more heavily into the chair.

b. As you relax, visualise yourself sitting in a place which is peaceful . . . You are comfortable, calm and there is no chance of your being disturbed . . . Where are you? Perhaps you are in the mountains or by the sea, in a forest or a meadow . . . A number of different places may possibly come to mind. Allow your imagination to settle in one place and allow other images to fade . . . Be aware of yourself sitting in this place . . . Be aware of how peaceful it is . . .

c. Looking straight ahead, begin to explore the things you can see in this place – the objects . . . colours . . . shapes . . . textures . . . and any movements that catch your eye . . . As you look ahead be aware of the season, the time of day and the weather . . . What signs of these things can you see? . . . Focus on the area immediately in front of you and then allow your eyes to wander to the far distance . . . and back again . . .

Now turn and look to the right . . . and again notice what you can see, what shapes, colours and textures . . . As you look become aware of the sounds that belong to this place . . . the sound of water perhaps, wind or of other elements . . . the sound of birds or other wildlife . . . Listen to the sounds both near and far away.

Now turn to the left . . . and again notice what you can see, what shapes, colours and textures . . . As you look take a deep breath through your nose and become aware of the smells that are carried in the air . . . Are they spicy, woody, floral, citrus? . . . Do the things that you can smell remind you of anything? . . . Allow your hands to feel the surface around you . . . Is it rough or smooth, hard or soft, warm or cool, damp or dry? . . .

Let your hands come to rest again and settle back into your original position, looking straight ahead into the distance . . .

d. Now let the scene fade for a moment and without opening your eyes become aware again of your body on the chair in this room . . . Feel the weight of your body in the chair and become particularly aware of your hands . . . In your own time, take the thumb of your left hand in the fingers of the right hand and squeeze your thumb with a gentle pressure . . . and as you feel

5 For many years we used the visualisation component of this exercise either as a means of inducing relaxation or as an introduction to a creative visualisation aimed specifically at releasing the imagination. The idea of developing the exercise to include the 'trigger' technique (see below) came from *Sporting Body, Sporting Mind* by John Syer and Christopher Connolly. This book confirmed our view that there are similarities in the challenges faced by the performer of sung theatre and the competitive athlete. You can use this exercise to withdraw temporarily from distractions. You may find it particularly helpful for dealing with sudden anxiety that can arise before a performance or an audition.

The object is to reduce anxiety to a point at which it no longer interferes with performance. You should practise it on a regular basis. Eventually the feeling it engenders can be triggered instantly without the need to go through the whole exercise. It is particularly useful for moments when you have little time in which to control your anxiety.

35

this pressure, let yourself drift back to the peaceful place you found . . .

Picture yourself there sitting looking straight ahead of you . . . allow yourself to become aware of the peacefulness in this place and the calm it is inducing in you . . . Looking straight ahead, begin again to explore the things you can see in this place – the objects . . . colours . . . shapes . . . textures . . . and any movements that catch your eye . . . Be aware once again of the season, the time of day and the weather . . . Focus once again on the area immediately in front of you and then allow your eyes to wander to the far distance . . . and back again . . .

e. Take a final look around and settle back into your original position looking straight ahead . . . In your own time you will decide to come back to the room again. As you do so, let go of your thumb and then open your eyes.

Holding your thumb as you go into the visualised place can be developed with practice into a 'trigger' technique. In time this will enable you to change places instantly for just the moment you need it, simply by closing your eyes and holding your thumb when the need for this calm arises.

Another variation of this exercise entitled 'Creating Your Sanctuary' appears in *Creative Visualization* by Shakti Gawain (pp. 68–9).

EXERCISE 4

Title: Black Box

Destination: To free the mind for rehearsal and performance

Via: Visualisation

Time Needed: 15 minutes

Risk: Low

Resources: None

Instructions[6]

Sit quietly, close your eyes, take a deep breath and allow yourself to settle heavily into your chair as you breathe out slowly. Imagine yourself sitting at a desk in front of a window. Look out and notice what you see, what the weather is

6 It is essential to clear away distractions once work begins. This exercise from *Sporting Body, Sporting Mind* represents one way to help yourself let go of distractions. Use it to prepare mentally for rehearsal or performance.

36

like, what movement there may be. Then look down at the desk and notice a blank sheet of paper and a pen. Pick up the pen and write down whatever is worrying or exciting you, anything you identify as a distraction. As you write, see the shape of your handwriting on the page, hear the point of your pen slide over the paper, feel the weight of your upper body on your arm. If you find it easier, you can draw a picture to represent the distractions or your distracted mood. When you have finished put down the pen, fold up the piece of paper and turn around. You see a box behind you. It may be on a shelf or on the floor. Notice how large it is, what colour it is, whether it is in the light or the shadow. Open the lid. Then put the folded piece of paper inside the box, close the lid and turn back to the desk, settling back into your chair and once more looking out of the window.

Having done this, you can open your eyes, ready to interact with those around you. However, it is important that once your session or match is over, you again close your eyes and go back to this imaginary desk, turn around, open the box, get out and unfold the piece of paper and look to see what you wrote or drew. Sometimes this will no longer be of interest and that's fine but, if the exercise is to continue to work – and with time it can become increasingly effective – the part of you that has been promised attention later on must learn to trust that it will get that attention.

(Syer and Connolly 1987: 14–15)

For the purposes of this exercise a distraction is anything that comes into your head which is not immediately concerned with your performance, rehearsal or audition on this day. Try rolling the piece of paper up as a parchment and tying it with a ribbon or picturing the box as an old chest with a big key that is then put in the drawer of the desk. If you do not find it helpful to imagine the script writing itself, adapt the exercise to suit the workings of your own imagination.

After a performance or audition the mind may well re-present the worries placed in the box. Some will no longer seem relevant in that they may have been born from the tension surrounding the performance in the first place. Others may have been taken care of by something that still goes on *in* the box.

WARMING-UP

Warming-up can be both a personal and a group process. It is more than just a physical and vocal awakening. It is more than a necessary chore to prevent damage through injury. Performing well means being physically, mentally and emotionally prepared for the extra-daily demands of your work. A thorough physical preparation helps you become more aware of what you are doing, thereby giving greater flexibility and control to change and respond. Group warm-ups also serve to attune members of the group to one another. A cast well attuned to each other and to the space in which they are to work (whether a rehearsal room or a theatre) will draw the most from the strengths of its individual members.

E X E R C I S E 5

Title: Physical Warm-up

Destination: To prepare the body and mind for rehearsal

Via: Physical awareness (fitness, flexibility and control)

Instructions

Singing and acting uses the whole body. The body's ability to respond is affected by your general level of fitness. A programme of regular exercise (aerobic) will improve breathing and your capacity to lower your heart rate, particularly at moments of stress. It is an essential part of building up the stamina necessary to perform night after night. For this reason you may find other training methods such as Tai Chi or martial arts effective ways of maintaining fitness, flexibility, control and general well-being.

The purpose of a physical warm-up before rehearsal or performance is first and foremost to prepare your body for the task that lies ahead. More specifically:

- Decreasing muscle tension and finding a relaxed physical state.
- Facilitating co-ordination by allowing for controlled and free use of the body.
- Facilitating your sense of balance and ability to control equilibrium.

- Increasing your range of movement.
- Preventing injury through muscle strain.
- Preparing the body and mind for activity.
- Developing an awareness of the body which may be used as a whole or in parts.

The range of activities you incorporate into a physical warm-up may include:

- Aerobic exercises that raise the heartbeat such as jogging, running on the spot, skipping and jumping. These are designed to get the heart and lungs working hard and should last about twelve minutes to give full benefit. At the end of these you should be breathing hard but not gasping for breath.
- Exercises that isolate different parts of the body. These are exercises where you concentrate on one part of the body at a time. For example: Head – tilting forward, side to side and rotating around in a circle. Shoulders – up and down, forward and back, etc. This process can be followed right through the body. Isolating two areas at a time involves the dissociation of one movement from another. For example, rotating the arms or shoulders in different directions, walking with one leg rigid and the other leg floppy or moving two hands independently from one another.
- Exercises for developing stamina and strength. These exercises involve working on particular groups of muscles, gradually building up their strength and improving their tone by repetition. For example, sit-ups, push-ups, chin-ups, flexing the ankle and foot, squeezing a ball many times to strengthen the fingers and hands. It is sensible not to begin with these exercises until the body is awakened, for example through stretching (see below).
- Exercises for cooling down. These are also important. When warming-up, the blood is pumped to all extremities of the body and if you stop suddenly then you may experience dizziness or stiffen up. Certain stretching routines are particularly useful when cooling down or indeed as part of the warm-up itself. Readers are referred to Bob Anderson's excellent book *Stretching* (see bibliography).

It is often helpful to start your physical warm-up lying on the floor. If your body is relaxed it should find a correct alignment and joints can be moved more easily.

It is also important to find a correct standing position with feet in a small 'V', knees pulled up but not locked, thighs pulled up but not tense, bottom down and under, stomach in and up, shoulders back and down and relaxed, arms hanging loosely by your sides, head up and eyes just above normal eye level.

Finally, when warming-up you should always start slowly and gently.

EXERCISE 6

Title: Vocal Warm-up

Destination: To prepare the voice for rehearsal

Instructions

The human voice is affected by external and internal conditions. External conditions are environmental, in particular the space and climate. Internal conditions are physical and psychological, in particular the morphology and muscular make-up of the body, health and state of mind.

It is important not to confuse preparing the voice for rehearsal with developing the vocal instrument. Both activities, however, use vocal exercises to achieve an end. Developing the vocal instrument is the particular speciality a singing teacher brings to the training of a performer. Amongst other things, a singing teacher should provide an effectively planned programme of singing exercises to be practised on a regular basis. The exercises below are not a substitute for this process. However, they outline some basic ideas for warming the voice up for rehearsal. In order to practise the exercises contained in this book you will have to accept your abilities and limitations as regards voice production and work on this aspect of your craft in parallel with the book.

A good vocal warm-up may include exercises that:

a. 'Balance' the voice vertically (see Figure 1, Figure 2). (For all figures see the Appendix).

b. 'Balance' the voice horizontally (see Figure 4, Figure 5, Figure 11) .

c. Arouse vibrations in the chest and head using sounds that create resonance (see Figure 2 and others where resonance creating consonants are incorporated).

d. Increase and strengthen the range of your voice (see Figure 6, Figure 8).

e. Improve control in attacking and sustaining notes (see Figure 5, Figure 9, Figure 10).

f. Warm-up the tongue, the lips, the jaw and the soft palate (see Figure 7, Figure 13). Also practise tongue twisters such as 'red leather, yellow leather', 'Peter Piper picked a peck of pickled peppers', 'the sixth sick sheikh's sixth sheep's sick', 'wicked cricket critic'.

g. Establish good intonation between intervals (see Figure 6, Figure 12).

h. Exercise the voice at different speeds for control and agility (see Figure 5, Figure 8, Figure 13).

i. Control dynamic changes (see Figure 9, Figure 10).

Of course an exercise can practise more than one of these areas at a time. However, it is necessary to be clear about exactly what aspect of technique you are looking at. Teachers, vocal coaches and books provide an endless source of vocal exercises. A good teacher will be able to create and adapt exercises to suit a performer's particular needs.

Vocal training necessarily takes place in circumstances very different to those on stage. However by integrating simple physical or imaginative activities into this training, you can prepare for the challenge of conditions on stage. It is essential to explore how your voice can be unbalanced by stage action away from the pressures of rehearsal. By integrating the following simple ideas into your vocal warm-up you can begin to find new balances which maintain a free voice during a prescribed activity.

Add any of the following ideas to a vocal warm-up exercise or invent some of your own:

- Describe a circle in the air with your left hand.
- Describe a square in the air with your right hand.
- Write your name in the air with each hand in turn.
- Balance on one leg.
- Shift your weight from one leg to the other.
- Lie down on your back, kneel or sit.
- Stand on tiptoes.
- Bend forward as if looking over a fence.
- Move your eyes to the left, to the right, upwards and downwards.
- Move your head to the left, to the right, slightly upwards and slightly downwards.
- Alternate your eye focus between an object close and an object far away.

- Throw an object into the air and catch it.
- Observe details about the space you are in. For example, the number of windows or the colour of the walls.
- Take your jacket or shoe off and put it on.
- Pull up a chair and sit down.
- Move around the room at different speeds and in different directions.
- Juggle.

Use your vocal warm-up exercises to translate imaginative ideas. Imagine any of the following and allow the thought or image of them to colour your voice:

- A cold, frosty day that turns into a warm, sunny day.
- The colour red that becomes white.
- Staring at the stars.
- A stream that becomes a waterfall.

These exercises should be practised slowly and executed free from unnecessary tension. If you start to feel tense then it is important to stop and rest. Begin again when you are relaxed.

ENERGISING

Energising is a process whereby you awaken or re-awaken your energy, ready to supply the mind and body in whatever way necessary. The performer's natural energy must be focused to serve expression in a precise way without losing any of the instinctive force behind it. Often we associate energy with tremendous vitality of movement based on speed and strength. However, it may also refer to something that is much more intimate, a power that pulses from within without dispersing. Your latent energy will need awakening – vocally, physically, psychologically – at the beginning of a working day. It is also worth bearing in mind that during the day (particularly following a protracted or very concentrated period of activity) there may be several points where your energy needs re-awakening. There are many exercises in this book that you can use depending on how you orientate them and on the particular energising you require. Here are some more general ideas.

EXERCISE 7

Title: Carwash

Destination: Energising through physical awakening

Via: Massage

Time Needed: 3+ minutes per person

Risk: Low/Medium

Resources: None

Instructions

a. Get into groups of five or six.

b. In each group everyone takes it in turns to stand in the centre of a circle formed by the other members of the group. The person in the centre either stands or flops forward and hangs gently from the waist. In either case you must close your eyes.

c. The rest of the group then massage that person's body, releasing all the muscle tones. Use repetitive movements around and across with the whole hand or the fingers. The fingers are appropriate for more delicate areas such as the neck, face, head and hands. In less sensitive areas such as the legs and arms the sides of the hands are more effective. Different members of the group work simultaneously on different parts of the body. When massaging take care to work thoroughly all over the body from the feet to the tips of the fingers. You are in effect combing the whole body for tensions.

d. When this process is finished bring the person being massaged gently to a standing position. Their eyes must remain closed.

e. Acting simultaneously as a group place your hands together over the head of the person being massaged. As if breaking an imaginary egg over this head, 'wash' their body with the palms of your hands in one firm fluid motion from the head down the body to the ground. Make sure that your hands do not lose contact with the body on their way down and that they pass from the feet to the ground.

Variation 1

A very simple and quick variation of this exercise is to find a partner and stand opposite them. Gently massage each other's face including the eyes.

43

7 This is a run-around game often played by children in the playground. Games such as this can release excess nervous energy and take the performer's mind away from their movements (another method for the release of tension). It is useful both for the physical activity involved and as a co-operation game, re-awakening our awareness of others.

8 If the group of catchers are co-operating well they will realise they must decide on an overall plan of action (i.e. tactics) if they are to stand any chance of achieving their objective.

9 This exercise works well as an energiser at the beginning of a workshop. It also explores dissociated activities, in this case, being open to receive one instruction while carrying out an activity demanded by another. The group should at all times be responsive to the leader's instructions and wherever possible maintain silence.

10 Discipline and precision are vital at this stage.

11 For further ideas refer to the eye-contact exercises in the section on Awareness. Another

EXERCISE 8

Title: Stuck in the Mud

Destination: Energising through physical release

Via: Movement and co-operation

Time Needed: 10 minutes

Risk: Low

Resources: None

Instructions[7]

a.   Choose two or more of the group to be 'it' (the catchers). Their objective is to catch everyone out.[8]

b.   The rest of the group must flee from the catchers. When caught you must stand still, legs apart and arms out to the sides.

c.   Other members of the group being chased can rescue those caught by passing through their legs. Those rescued are then free to rescue others and participate in the game.

EXERCISE 9

Title: Milling

Destination: Energising

Via: Movement, listening and reacting, awareness

Time Needed: 15+ minutes

Risk: Low

Resources: None

Instructions[9]

a.   Move around the room listening for a series of simple physical instructions from a leader, which you must immediately undertake. For example, 'stop', 'go', 'change direction'.[10]

b.   Incorporate awareness into this activity. For example, whilst moving in the space establish positive contact with each other. For example, making eye-contact and saying 'hello' or shaking hands.[11]

c. Incorporate other areas of discipline into the activity described in step a. Some practical ideas are:

- Move as far apart as possible from every other person without leaving the space and moving as close as possible to every other person without physically touching. As you are actually moving as far or as near as possible from *every* other person there should not be a point where you actually stop.
- Touch anyone who . . . (is wearing blue, has short hair, etc).
- Find someone who . . . (has the same hand size, listens to the same music, etc).
- Connect to someone by parts of the body . . . (elbows, knees, noses, etc).
- Form sculptural shapes with the body . . . (geometric shapes such as squares and circles; group pictures such as 'Famous Monument', 'The Execution', etc).
- Form a straight line from the tallest to smallest, darkest eyes to lightest eyes, most organised to least organised, most courageous to least courageous, most agree with a given statement to least agree with that statement, etc.[12]
- Move as if subject to different weather conditions; move on different surfaces and through different zones in the room; move to different pieces of music.

d. Incorporate a sung call and response activity (see Figure 20, Figure 21) into the activity described in step a.

During any of the above tasks the leader may issue a simple physical instruction (see step a). React to this instruction without hesitation.[13]

E X E R C I S E   1 0

Title: Points on the Floor

Destination: Energising through co-operation

Via: Co-operation, imagination

Time Needed: 10 minutes

Risk: Low

Resources: None

Instructions

a. Divide into smaller groups of six or seven.

awareness activity is for the group to observe as many details about the room as possible. This can be tested at any point during the exercise by asking the group to stop, close their eyes and answer specific questions. For example, how many light fittings are there?

12 This may involve some negotiation and therefore take longer to work through.

13 This is about conditioning the mind and body to remain open to the possibility of another instruction without this affecting the quality of the task being undertaken at the time.

b. Each part of your body that touches the floor is worth one point. Thus two feet touching the floor is worth a total of two points. Two elbows and two feet touching the floor is worth four points. And so on. If five fingers are placed on the floor then this is worth five points. If, however, the palm of your hand is placed flat on the floor with fingers tight together then this is worth one point. Also, for the sake of argument, if you lie flat on the floor with legs together then this is worth one point also.

c. In your group make the number of points called out by the leader and present this in the form of a group sculpture that is as weird and bizarre as possible. This sculpture must also physically connect each member of your group in some way.[14]

14 Any number of points can be called, though it is helpful to work down from a high number to a low number. The leader may or may not take the time to verify the number of points made.

Variation 1

The game above can be played in exactly the same way except that you are not allowed to talk during any of the process.

EXERCISE 11

Title: 'La Donna è Mobile'

Destination: Energising the voice

Via: Co-ordinating singing and movement

Time Needed: 10+ minutes

Risk: Medium/low

Resources: A piano is useful but not essential

Instructions

This exercise contains a sequence of movements with four beats in a bar and a song with three beats in a bar.

a. Learn the melody of Verdi's 'La donna è mobile' (Figure 18) to the word 'la'.

b. Learn the following sequence of movements (Figure 19):

    Beat 1   Hop forward on the left foot
    Beat 2   Hop forward on the left foot
    Beat 3   Back onto the right foot
    Beat 4   Clap over the head

c. Line up against a wall.

d. After a count of either three or four sing the song whilst attempting the sequence of movements. Repeat the song and movements until you reach the other side of the room.[15]

EXERCISE 12

Title: The Invisible Ball

Destination: Energising the mind, body, voice relationship

Via: Imagination, sustaining vocal energy, transforming and channelling energy

Time Needed: 15+ minutes

Risk: Medium

Resources: None

Instructions[16]

a. Form a circle. The object of the exercise is to pass an invisible ball from person to person (in no particular order).

b. Try building the exercise in the following stages:

  i Pass a ball of the same weight from person to person at different speeds and different heights. Of particular importance here is that the line of your body suggests the path of the ball.

  ii Mark the path of the ball with a vocal sound when you throw it. This starts when the ball leaves the thrower's hand and stops when it reaches the catcher's hand.

  iii When you catch the ball, keep its energy alive in the body and transform this energy through the body before releasing the ball again on a new path. Thus a very fast, direct ball may send the catcher's body into a spin. The catcher must find a way of converting this physical energy (the spin) into a new physical expression. When you have found this, release the imaginary ball on its new path to another member of the group. This stage of the exercise takes place without vocal sounds.

  iv Next re-introduce vocalised sound not only to mark the path of the ball but also the transformation of its energy

16 Repeat this exercise regularly. It will energise the mental, physical and vocal dynamic, particularly after the isolated warming-up of different areas. Make clear eye-contact (see Awareness).

47

through the body. In other words, as the catcher you must also catch the sound and transform its energy.

17 This variation encourages you to dissociate the physical and vocal dynamic within the same activity.

Variation 1[17]

The elements of the exercise above remain the same except that the physical dynamic marks one path of the ball whilst the vocal dynamic is not equivalent but marks another possible path of the ball. As the catcher you must be open to receive the separate physical and vocal energies. In the final stage of the exercise this will involve maintaining their separateness as each is transformed before being released to another member of the circle.

EXERCISE 13

Title: Percentages

Destination: Finding a physical expression of energy

Via: Internalised memory of movement and externalised physical expression

Time Needed: 30+ minutes

Risk: Low

Resources: None

18 This exercise uses a much-simplified version of basic movement qualities derived from the work of Rudolf Laban. These can be combined in different ways to explore physical and vocal language. They are useful for exploring characterisation (see Chapter 5) and helping a performer recognise physical habits. Here they are used as part of the energising process.

Instructions[18]

a. Explore each of the following movement qualities in isolation and in as many different ways as possible (for example, performing different actions such as travelling through space, jumping and turning, moving in relation to different people or objects and using the space in different ways such as high, medium and low levels, on the spot or near or far away):

- *Direct movement* For example, choose a point and move towards it; stop directly; turn directly and choose another point.
- *Flexible movement* For example, close your eyes and follow the sound of a partner's clicking finger. Open your eyes and follow their moving hand across a space. Being 'flexible' is about perpetually finding a journey, always changing direction.
- *Strong use of weight* For example, imagine yourself

48

composed of lead, beginning to move through a sea of oil. There is an internal sense of weight and an external resistance.

- *Light use of weight* For example, imagine yourself composed of helium, moved by a slight breeze that gets steadily stronger.
- *Fast or sudden use of time* Remember that this is not absolute but capable of variation.
- *Slow use of time* Remember that this is not absolute but capable of variation.

The aim is to situate the qualities described above in the body in such a way that the memory of them is secure. Later you will be asked to recall the feeling of an activity without physically executing it.

Find each quality in your body both successively (one part after another) and simultaneously (all parts together).

Remember that none of the qualities are absolute. In other words movements may be more or less direct, light etc. Introduce the idea of percentages as a way of exploring variations in the dynamic of each movement quality. The greater a percentage the more direct, light etc. the quality of movement must become. Do different percentages naturally give rise to ideas for different movement activities? For example, standing, sitting, walking, looking out the window, opening a door, etc?

b. Next recall the feeling of each activity without physically executing it (internalised memory of movement).

Repeat steps a and b several times, if necessary. You may find it helpful to move to stage b after working on each movement quality (direct, flexible, etc).

c. Now introduce percentages to experience the transition from an internalised to an externalised expression of energy. 1 per cent represents the most internalised physical expression of energy and 100 per cent the most externalised physical expression of energy.[19]

Variation 1

Explore the stages of the exercise defined above as expressed in the hands alone and in the eyes alone.

19 It may be helpful before this stage of the exercise to divide the group into two with one half observing.

Variation 2

Explore the stages of the exercise defined above incorporating a vocal exercise or song. Use the idea of percentages to encourage the characterisation of your sound, and gradually practise combining different physical states with singing. See how exaggerated your movement qualities can become whilst maintaining a free column of air.

EXERCISE 14

Title: The Telephone Game

Destination: Energising the voice

Via: Singing

Time Needed: 10+ minutes

Risk: Low

Resources: None

20 This is a simple call and response game where small solos are shared among group members. It can be played in a circle or incorporated into an exercise like 'Milling'.

Instructions[20]

a.   Learn Figure 20. One member of the group is 'telephoned' first. We have used 'Betty' as an example.

b.   The group member chosen in the first bar of the song replies in the second bar. For example:

Group: Hey Betty!
Betty: I think I hear my name.
Group: Hey Betty!
Betty: I think I hear it again.
Group: You're wanted on the telephone.
Betty: If it's not Barney (*the soloist nominates the next soloist from the group*) then I'm not at home.
Group: With a rick tick tickety tick, oh yeah, with a rick tick tickety tick.
Group: Hey Barney!
Barney: I think I hear my name . . . (*and so on*).

If someone does not reply, you must as a group keep singing 'Hey (name)!' until he or she replies.

CONCENTRATION

Concentration has been defined as a withdrawal of attention from factors that are no longer or have never been relevant to your immediate performance so that you can be receptive to those that are. Everything you do demands concentration. It is the discipline that leads to focus. Singing and acting at the same time requires an extra-daily precision and maintaining of focus due, as we have said, to the level of co-ordination involved. As you improve this co-ordination so the range of musical and dramatic choices available to you increase as will your power to communicate with clarity the musical and dramatic choices you make.

Essential to concentration is the exclusion of unwanted external and internal interference. For example, noises backstage, coughing in the audience or the self-critical 'inner voice'. As important, however, is incorporating necessary external influences. For example, the energy of a conductor or other characters.

Never force concentration as this creates tension. Rather practise it. Many performers have unhelpful patterns of thought and behaviour that are deeply embedded. With practice these patterns can be broken. The greater your level of concentration, the more aware you will become. The converse is also true. The more aware you are, the easier you will find it to incorporate spontaneity into your performance.

Use the following exercises in conjunction with the exercises based on awareness to be found in the next section.

E X E R C I S E   1 5

Title: Concentration (Solo 1)

Destination: To prepare the mind for rehearsal

Via: Listening

Time Needed: 15+ minutes

Risk: Low

Resources: A mat, a quiet warm place

Instructions

a. Sit yourself comfortably on a mat and close your eyes. Place two fingers on different pulse points in turn, for example, the temples, the neck, the wrist, the groin.

b.   At each of these points 'listen' to the beat of your pulse and allow your breathing to settle.

c.   When you have achieved this and worked your way through the pulse points, lie back on the mat keeping your eyes closed.

d.   Listen initially to the sounds that are close at hand, in the immediate vicinity (the buzzes, resonances, murmurs, creaks, rattles, hums and drones).

e.   Gradually extend the range of your hearing to sounds that are farther and farther away. As you do so, make a mental note of the different sounds you can hear.

f.   Next work your way back gradually to the sounds immediately around you.

g.   Finally repeat the exercise but this time focus on each sound in turn for a little longer. Take the time to consider each sound and ask yourself questions as you listen to it: Is it steady? Does it have a rhythm to it? Does it change pitch? How would you describe the texture of the sound? Focus only on the qualities of each sound as you attune your hearing to it.

h.   When you are ready, open your eyes and sit up.

E X E R C I S E   1 6

Title: Concentration (Solo 2)

Destination: Practising concentration

Via: Observation, stimulation of the senses

Time Needed: 10 minutes

Risk: Low

Resources: An object or picture, an alarm clock or timer

Instructions

a.   Set the alarm clock or timer to ring in five minutes and sit comfortably in a chair in front of an object or a picture that is unfamiliar to you.

b.   Attend fully to the object or picture, observing its many qualities (shapes, colours, textures). Observe first from a general point of view (the whole picture) and then from an increasingly detailed point of view (the smallest details of the picture). When the alarm rings then close your eyes.

c. Picture as many details in your mind's eye as possible. When you have finished, open your eyes and compare your mental images to the original stimulus.[21]

E X E R C I S E   1 7

Title: Pass the Pig
Destination: Concentration
Via: Listening
Time Needed: 10 minutes
Risk: Low
Resources: None

Instructions

a. Form a circle and stand in a relaxed position, arms by your sides.

b. A leader begins by saying someone else's name three times during which time the said person must say their name once.

c. If they say their name once before the leader has finished then the leader must continue until someone fails to say their name in time. When this happens, that person takes over as leader.[22]

E X E R C I S E   1 8

Title: Oh Balls!
Destination: Concentration, awareness
Via: Eye-contact
Time Needed: 15+ minutes
Risk: Low
Resources: A minimum of three soft juggling balls

Instructions[23]

a. Stand in a circle in a relaxed position.

21 When you are familiar with this exercise try dispensing with the clock and rely on yourself to provide an internal clock. Be aware of attending fully to the object without allowing yourself to be distracted by the time question.

22 This exercise is not just about encouraging you to be alert. It also develops the technique of quick group refocus after a disruption. In this case, when someone fails to say their name, the focus of the group often dissipates through a release of tension in the form of laughter. This idea of refocus is explored further in the next exercise.

23 This exercise must build from the skills of basic eye-contact exercises such as 'Crossing the Circle' (Awareness).

b.   Introduce one ball into the circle by making eye-contact with someone and throwing the ball under control across the circle for him or her to catch.

c.   The ball is thrown from person to person only after eye-contact has been established.

d.   When this is flowing smoothly then introduce another ball and then eventually another ball until all three balls are being thrown across the circle by different people at the same time.[24]

e.   Whenever a ball is dropped (which every member of the group should immediately be aware of), the person who dropped it shouts: 'Oh balls!' The game must pause immediately whether or not other balls are in the air. When everyone has refocused the game recommences.[25]

Variation 1

When catching the ball you must make a 360-degree turn before doing so. This increases the levels of physical co-ordination and awareness necessary in this exercise.[26]

EXERCISE 19

Title: Group Clap

Destination: Concentration

Via: Awareness

Time Needed: 10 minutes

Risk: Low

Resources: None

Instructions[27]

a.   Form a circle and stand in a relaxed position.

b.   Everyone holds their arms out to the side in such a way that each person's middle finger is touching the next person's middle finger. In this way the whole group is connected fingertip to fingertip.

c.   The object of the exercise is for everyone in the group to clap at the same time.[28]

24 At this stage encourage fluidity and flexibility in the play and swift eye-contact.

25 Shouting this expletive is a simple way to prevent mistakes building up. During performance a momentary lapse of concentration can easily have a cumulative effect if the performer begins to ruminate on the original mistake. Only by letting go of a mistake will the cycle be broken.

26 Further variations and ways of building this important game appear in the next section (Awareness).

27 Although this exercise principally draws upon and stimulates a group's awareness, it is also an excellent game when a quick focus is needed.

28 At the beginning the leader may facilitate by leading the clap in some way, for example, suggesting a form of upbeat such as an audible breath. After a while it should be possible for everyone to clap at the same time without such an intervention.

EXERCISE 20

Title: A Fork . . . A Spoon?

Destination: Sustained concentration

Via: Listening, spatial awareness

Time Needed: 10+ minutes

Risk: Low

Resources: A fork and a spoon

Instructions[29]

a. Stand in a circle.

b. A leader, who has a fork in their right hand and a spoon in their left hand, turns to the person immediately on their right side ('A') and says, 'This is a fork'. 'A' in turn replies, 'A what?' The leader replies, 'A fork' and passes it to them.

c. 'A' then turns to the person on *their* right ('B') and says, 'This is a fork'. 'B' in turn replies, 'A what?' and 'A' repeats, 'A what?' to the leader who replies, 'A fork'. This message ('a fork') is then passed (with the fork) from 'A' to 'B' who then turns to the person on their right ('C') and says, 'This is a fork'. The process continues as described above from one member of the group to the next with 'A what?' and 'A fork' being passed backwards and forwards each time to and from the leader.

d. Once this is established then the leader begins the same process with the spoon on their left side. The only difference is that the word 'spoon' is used instead of 'fork'.

e. Continue until the fork and spoon have travelled around the circle (swapping over at some point) and ended up in the hands of the leader again. The fork and spoon never travel backwards down the line even though the line 'A what?' does.

29 This exercise tests concentration over an extended period.

EXERCISE 21

Title: Don't Blame Me

Destination: Concentrated pitching

Via: Singing, pitching, aural awareness, co-ordination

Time Needed: 10+ minutes

Risk: Low

Resources: A pitched instrument may be necessary for the variations.

30 This is another 'rubbing your stomach and patting your head' style of game. The demands on concentration are greater in the variations. Use it to develop aural awareness and pitching.

Instructions[30]

a.   Get into groups of between four and eight. We use a group of six here as an example.

b.   Standing in a circle, each group member sings a successive note of a scale, starting from the first person's note and going upwards in pitch. It is helpful at this stage to attach the appropriate word *Do, Re, Mi, Fa, So* to each note.

c.   In a group of six, only the first five notes of the scale are sung. The sixth member of the group goes back to the pitch at the beginning, singing *Do*. Therefore when the singing passes round the circle for a second time the first person sings *Re* (see below).

1	2	3	4	5	6	1	2
Do	Re	Mi	Fa	So	Do	Re	Mi

3	4	5	6	1	2	3	4
Fa	So	Do	Re	Mi	Fa	So	Do

If the number in each group is five then use either the first four notes of the scale or the first six notes.

d.   Try to keep a steady rhythm. Begin slowly.

Variation 1

Repeat the above exercise singing all notes to *La*.

Variation 2

Replace certain notes with sounds or gestures (clicking fingers, clapping, stamping). For example, instead of singing the third note of the scale you must click your fingers. The following person continues the sequence as if the note has been sung. Replace another note, sound or gesture.

Variation 3

Instead of using the major scale, use other sequences. For example, a minor scale, broken chords, or devise your own simple sequence.

Variation 4

Use words with the notes but have one less word than there are notes. For example, in a group of six there would be five notes and four words. The words could form a phrase. For example, 'Where have you been?' It may be helpful to speak the text first and then re-introduce pitch at a later stage.

EXERCISE 22

Title: Guess the Leader

Destination: Concentration

Via: Observation

Time Needed: 10 minutes

Risk: Low

Resources: None

Instructions:

a.   Sit in a circle.

b.   Choose someone in the group to stand some way off with their back to the rest of the group.

c.   Next silently choose a leader from within the group.

d.   The leader begins a sequence of repeated actions (for example, clapping or tapping a part of the body). The actions themselves change at regular intervals. The group must copy these actions at exactly the same time and in exactly the same way.

e.   Once this pattern has been established, the person with their back to the group is called. He or she turns around and tries to guess who is leading the sequence.

f.   When the leader is discovered then this person must position themselves with their back to the group and the person who had been guessing will choose another leader before joining the circle.

EXERCISE 23

Title: Clapping While Telling a Story

Destination: Concentration

Via: Rhythm, imagination

Time Needed: 15 minutes

Risk: Low

Resources: None

Instructions

a. Sit in a circle and establish a pulse whereby each person in the circle claps one after the other.

b. When the pulse is flowing smoothly a leader announces (somewhat deceitfully) that they have a story in their head that the group must guess by asking questions.

c. Each member of the circle takes it in turn (going in a direction opposite to the clapping) to ask a question that the leader can answer with a 'yes' or 'no'. For example: Does the story take place in contemporary times? Does it concern someone they know? Does it concern a man? Is he in love? These questions have no fixed rhythm (normal speech).

d. The leader replies either 'yes' or 'no' to the questions.[31]

e. When the last person in the circle has asked a question, the story stops, as does the clapping.

Variation 1

You can tell any story during the above exercise. One possibility is 'the good news is . . . the bad news is' format which alternates from person to person.

31 The leader's answers serve simply to keep the story emerging. The choice of 'yes' or 'no' will be arbitrary, even though the questioners do not know this.

AWARENESS

The performer of sung theatre needs a level of awareness that incorporates the many different facets of performance, from the spontaneous feelings and reactions of other performers in character to the externals of design. Awareness between characters is particularly important so that you are not simply singing *at* each other but communicating in such a way that you elicit reactions from one another, mentally, physically and emotionally. In this way awareness contributes to spontaneity.

Many of the exercises that follow focus on performing two or more activities at the same time. This is one way to develop the concentration necessary not just to exclude unwanted influences but also to open the mind to managing different tasks simultaneously. Often as one channel of awareness opens another closes, albeit momentarily. This can result in a loss of clarity in any area of performance. For example, you may come out of character or sing an inappropriate musical dynamic. Practising these exercises will lead to a more open awareness. This is beautiful to watch and joyful to experience.

EXERCISE 24

Title: Humbling Along

Destination: Group awareness

Via: Vocal improvisation

Time Needed: 5 minutes

Risk: Low

Resources: None

Instructions[32]

a. Place chairs around the room in no particular order or pattern. The precise number of chairs should equal the number of participants minus one.

b. As a group, congregate in one corner. On a given signal you sit down on the chairs as quickly as possible. However, you must walk with your knees pressed together (or tied at the ankles with a scarf) and you must hum your own tune which you make up while you are walking.

32 A quick and easy warm-up game.

59

33 This exercise is well known. Use it as a basic starter game or a refresher.

34 Encourage the group to use the whole space. Stop regularly to assess how well the group has succeeded in occupying every space. The more evenly spaced each person is the better.

35 Only introduce the variations if the group is comfortable with the initial exercise.

36 Make sure progress already made in filling the space is not lost now that people are no longer thinking merely in terms of themselves.

Eye-contact may cause more background noise. Even though everyone will be saying 'hello', the aim is to maintain the same focus that existed when everyone was silent.

37 While the different environmental conditions will affect the nature of the greeting, make sure eye-contact is not lost and clarity of focus is maintained.

This exercise is particularly useful for the practice of chorus work where individual initiative is needed for a chorus to communicate through their use of space.

EXERCISE 25

Title: Finding the Space

Destination: Spatial awareness

Via: Concentration, co-operation, eye-contact

Time Needed: 15 minutes

Risk: Low

Resources: None

Instructions[33]

a.   Walk around the room in silence, moving into an empty space whenever and wherever one becomes vacant. The moment you have arrived in this space you may pause for a moment but must then move on immediately to another vacant space.

b.   When the leader stops the game, everyone must 'freeze' in his or her position.[34]

c.   Repeat stages a–b as necessary.

Variation 1[35]

Move off again as above only this time when moving you must try to make eye-contact with as many other people in the group as possible. When you do so you must greet that person with the word 'Hello!'[36]

Variation 2

When you move off again, move as if subject to different weather conditions – light rain, heavy rain, hailstorm, snow blizzard in high winds, warm day, blazing hot day, etc.[37]

EXERCISE 26

Title: Tribe

Destination: Group awareness

Via: Movement, trust

Time Needed: 10 minutes

Risk: Low

Resources: None

Instructions

a. The object of the exercise is to move around the space at the same speed as everyone else in the group. When you begin the exercise, move at a 'normal' walking pace. From then on the pace of movement can speed up or slow down. However, if there is a change in speed it must be because the group as a unit or tribe has made an unspoken decision to move faster or slower.[38]

b. Discuss your reactions to this exercise. Was it easy or difficult to avoid taking an individual decision to change the speed? Were you aware of anyone who was doing so? Did you feel a pressure to initiate a change of speed? At what moments was the pressure to 'go it alone' the greatest? How comfortable were you when no changes of speed took place?

38 To play this game you need to let go of your individual impulses, subordinating them to the will of the group. At no time in the exercise must a group member take an individual decision to change the speed.

EXERCISE 27

Title: Concert

Destination: Aural awareness

Via: Rhythm, vocal improvisation, relaxation

Time Needed: 15+ minutes

Risk: Low/medium

Resources: None

Instructions

a. Lie back on the floor (knees raised so that the soles of your feet are firmly on the ground) with your head towards the centre of the group circle and your feet away from the centre.

b. At a signal from the leader each member of the group vocalises an 'Ah' sound at any pitch.

c. When you no longer have enough breath to sustain your note then take a new breath and vocalise again on a different pitch.

d. When the leader says the word 'Concert!' then as a group you must find your way to a single note.

e. When the leader says the word 'Concert!' again, on the next breath you take return to stage b.[39]

39 Resist the temptation to lead the other members of the group. The decision as to what note eventually emerges is taken by the group itself. This requires considerable trust and openness, as well as letting go of your own desire to control.

40 There is no hurry to arrive at a unison.

41 Return to this simple game to reinforce its skill. Eye-contact is a fundamental building block of awareness. It is a physical manifestation of focus and is linked to other areas of clarity, for example, diction, emotion and musical dynamic.

42 Watch out for newer members of the group or visiting guests. If these people are being neglected, stop the game and point this out.

Inevitably people will first make eye-contact with those opposite. Stop the game. Encourage people to use their peripheral vision and switch with those on either side.

Feedback at the end of this game. There are usually one or two people who have made eye-contact with someone who has then turned away to look for someone else (i.e. avoided eye-contact) or broken eye-contact when crossing the circle. Discuss the issues of trust inherent in eye-contact before playing the game again.

Variation 1

Sit facing one another in a circle for this variation. Instead of vocalising a sound, each group member invents a different rhythm (for example, by clapping) and on the word 'Concert!' you must find your way to a single rhythm. On the word 'concert' again the group rhythm breaks down as each of you returns to your original rhythm.[40]

EXERCISE 28

Title: Crossing the Circle

Destination: Eye-contact

Via: Concentration

Time Needed: 10 minutes

Risk: Low

Resources: None

Instructions[41]

a. As a group form a circle. Stand comfortably with arms relaxed by your sides. Make sure that the circle is perfectly round so that you can see everyone else.

b. When the game begins you must make eye-contact with someone else in the circle. Having done so you both immediately cross the circle in a straight line. Move towards each other maintaining eye-contact for as long as possible as you pass one another and swap places.

c. When you have swapped places you must try and make eye-contact with someone else in the circle and move on. There is no limit to the number of people crossing the circle at any one time although you will need to move at different speeds to avoid any jam in the middle of the circle as you cross. Remember nevertheless to walk in a straight line. Finally, this exercise must be done in complete silence.[42]

Variation 1

Move around the room and when you make eye-contact with someone else imagine that there is an invisible piece of elastic that binds you together and that stretches between you. Explore the space between you moving nearer and then further away, higher and lower whilst all the time maintaining eye-contact. If the contact with your partner is broken for whatever reason then you must break the imaginary elastic and find another partner.

Variation 2

Get into pairs and decide on an 'A' and a 'B'. 'A' is the leader and 'B' is the follower. 'A' and 'B' stand opposite one another about a metre apart. As a leader you must hold the palm of your hand flat out in front of you. As a follower you must keep your face at the same distance from the leader's hand during the course of the exercise. The leaders then execute a series of movements with their raised hand. Start from a stationary position and then move around the space. Whilst you are not trying to catch your partner out, you should nevertheless experiment with your hand being at different levels and angles to the ground. After a period of time the leader and follower may swap roles.

Variation 3

As above only this time the leader is guiding two people, one with each hand. The leader must not stop moving either hand. The two followers must not touch at any point. After a period of time, swap roles so that each follower takes it in turn to lead. Begin slowly.

EXERCISE 29

Title: Changing Notes

Destination: Melodic awareness

Via: Listening, imagination, pitching

Time Needed: 10 minutes

Risk: Medium

Resources: None

Instructions[43]

a. Person 'A' sings a three note melody. It should be a melody that everyone can sing.

b. Person 'B' sings a melody that uses two of the notes from the

43 A simple game that combines precise listening with a minimal amount of improvisation.

previous melody but changes one of them. Any one of the three notes may be changed.

c. Person 'C' sings a melody that uses two notes from 'B's melody and changes one of them.[44]

44 It is easier to change either the first or third notes. Changing the middle note is more difficult as it demands an act of imagination between two acts of precision. If participants change the same note in the sequence each time then make a requirement that a different note in the sequence be changed each time.

EXERCISE 30

Title: Passing a Note

Destination: Co-ordination of a dramatic and musical task

Via: Listening, pitching, breath control, timing, eye-contact

Time Needed: 10 minutes

Risk: Medium

Resources: None

45 You will need to have played 'Crossing the Circle'.

Instructions[45]

a. Person 'A' sings a note.

b. 'A' makes eye-contact with someone in the circle ('B').

c. 'A' and 'B' swap places. 'A' keeps singing until he or she walks past 'B'. At the moment the two pass each other, 'B' takes over the singing from 'A', singing the same note as 'A'.

d. When 'B' reaches the other side of the circle, he or she makes eye-contact with someone else ('C'), and they exchange places as above.[46]

46 This game is best played in a group of eight to twelve. The person singing should complete the required task in one breath. This is difficult at first. Tighter circles make the game easier in relation to breath control, but call for greater concentration and precision in making eye-contact.

During this exercise pay attention to the following areas:

• Maintaining alertness through visual and aural awareness of the person who is singing.
• Registering eye-contact.
• Moving when the other person moves.
• Listening to the note being sung and pitching it in your head.
• Timing your breath. Breathing too early creates too long a suspension at the top of the inhalation thereby causing tension. Breathing too late will either mean the beginning of the note is late or the breath is too shallow to achieve the exercise.
• Maintaining the quality of singing while exchanging places.
• Maintaining the quality of singing while eye-contact with another person is established.

EXERCISE 31

Title: Eye-contact Chords

Destination: Harmonic awareness

Via: Singing, pitching, listening, eye-contact

Time Needed: 10+ minutes

Risk: Low/medium

Resources: A piano or any pitched instrument

Instructions[47]

a.   A leader plays a three-note chord, for example, F, A, C (F major triad). You must remember all three notes.

b.   Person 'A' sings any note from the triad.

c.   Person 'A' makes eye-contact with someone in the circle ('B').

d.   'A' and 'B' exchange places. The moment 'A' and 'B' walk past one another, 'B' sings a different note from the triad.

e.   'A' keeps singing until he or she reaches the edge of the circle.

f.   When 'B' reaches the edge of the circle, he or she makes eye-contact with someone else in the circle ('C').

g.   'B' and 'C' exchange places. Repeat as above.[48]

[47] This game uses a similar approach to the previous exercise.

EXERCISE 32

Title: Zombie Dead

Destination: Eye-contact

Via: Trust, awareness, concentration

Time Needed: 10 minutes

Risk: Medium

Resources: None

Instructions

a.   Form a circle, standing comfortably.

b.   Person 'A' plays the zombie with arms outstretched in the style of a cod horror film and proceeds to walk from the centre of the

[48] This exercise is musically more difficult than the previous one although the aspects of co-ordination are similar. Additional areas of attention include: maintaining aural awareness of the note being sung and the notes available should eye-contact be made; listening to the note being sung and choosing the note you would like to sing by pitching it 'in your head'; maintaining the pitch once the other person starts to sing a different note.

49 Discuss the issues of trust that arise from this game as they directly affect the level of responsibility performers are prepared to accept with respect to each other on stage. Person 'B' is under pressure and must make clear eye-contact with someone. The rest of the group must be alert and willing to make eye-contact with 'B'. Social familiarity is also at issue here and the exercise is likely to flow more smoothly with a group who have been working together for a while.

However much members of the group may wish to support each other, no one is allowed to call out a name unless they are in eye-contact with the 'victim' as the zombie walks towards them. Using the example above, only 'C' has the right to call out 'B's name.

50 This exercise builds on the skills of 'Oh Balls!' and 'Crossing the Circle'. It is also useful for exploring the passing and receiving of focus on stage, particularly over greater distances.

circle towards a particular individual ('B') with whom they make eye-contact. The eye-contact is reinforced by the outstretched arms.

c. Person 'B' must make eye-contact with someone else in the circle ('C'). 'C' must say 'B's name before 'A' reaches 'B'.

d. If 'C' succeeds, 'A' continues playing the zombie, returning via the centre of the circle and picking a new target.

e. If 'A' reaches 'B' before 'C' calls out the name of 'B', then 'B' becomes the new zombie, and 'A' returns to the circle.[49]

EXERCISE 33

Title: Catch!

Destination: Awareness

Via: Eye-contact, concentration

Time Needed: 15+ minutes

Risk: Low

Resources: A minimum of two soft juggling balls and a maximum of one for every four members of the group. Variation 2 requires one long pole (a broom handle is ideal) per two members of the group.

Instructions[50]

a. Get into teams of four and form a small square.

b. Throw the ball from person to person within your group only after eye-contact has been established.

c. When this is flowing smoothly, introduce another ball so that two balls are being thrown within your group by different people at the same time.

d. As in Exercise 18, if you drop a ball then you must shout 'Oh balls!' and the game must pause. When everyone is concentrating again then you may recommence.

e. When this is flowing smoothly then move freely around the room passing the ball between members of your group over greater and lesser distances.

f. When this is flowing smoothly then play the game in this manner as one group. Experiment throwing the ball at different speeds, at different levels, over different distances and with varying lengths in between catching and throwing again.[51]

Variation 1

This variation uses long poles. The peripheral vision required will sharpen your receptiveness to the energy and movements of a conductor.

Find a partner and together find your own space in the room. Stand facing your partner across a small gap. Practise throwing the pole to each other across the gap in a trajectory that keeps the pole vertical in the air. As you become more confident with this you can widen the space between you, though not beyond what is comfortable in the throwing and catching of the stick.

When you are comfortable with this team up with another pair and in a small square pass the poles between you in any order having of course first made eye-contact with the person you are throwing to.

Finally as a team of four move freely around the space seeking to pass the two poles between members of your team as fluidly and efficiently as possible whilst always keeping on the move.

Variation 2

Get into groups of between five and eight. Arrange yourselves in a circle with one person in the middle. Two or more sticks are passed to the person in the middle, though not of course at the same time as a stick can only be thrown when eye-contact has been made between the person throwing and the person catching. Having caught a stick the person in the middle throws it back out to another point in the circle.[52]

EXERCISE 34

Title: The Conductor

Destination: Awareness, vocal improvisation

Via: Imagination, co-operation, clarity, co-ordination of gesture

Time Needed: 15+ minutes

Risk: Medium

Resources: None

51 Always build up from one ball at the beginning of each variation of the game. As the game expands into the space, people may try and use their voices to make contact rather than their eyes. If this happens, reinforce the need for silence.

52 The same principle regarding letting go of mistakes applies in these variations.

Instructions

In this exercise a group reacts musically to visual information communicated by a conductor. The conductor's gestures need to be explained at the beginning of the exercise.

- When the conductor raises his or her arm, the pitch of your singing goes up. When the conductor lowers his or her arm, you lower the pitch of your singing.
- When the conductor's thumb and fingers are touching (shaped like the beak of a bird), sing an 'Oo'. When the conductor's thumb and fingers are fully open, sing an 'Ah'. One could say that the shape of the hand when conducting mirrors the shape of your mouth when singing.
- When the conductor closes his or her fist, then stop singing.
- When the conductor draws his or her hand closer to the body then the volume decreases.
- When the conductor stretches his or her arm out from the body, the volume increases.[53]

53 These signs do not need to be learned at once. It is possible to begin using only the first two commands.

a.   Get into two lines and stand either side of the conductor. He or she will communicate musical choices using both left and right arms. The left arm conducts all those individuals to the left and the right arm conducts all those to the right.

b.   Each piece begins and ends with the conductor crossing his or her arms over their chest.

c.   The conductor creates a piece of music with both arms using the gestures outlined above and experimenting with variations in pitch, volume, vowel sound and silence. The conductor must endeavour to communicate these choices clearly to the group, who must react with precision.

54 This variation builds in the skill of maintaining peripheral vision (in this case being aware of the conductor while performing a simple task).

Variation 1[54]

You are now free to move anywhere in the space although you should be aware of which of the conductor's hands you are following. Combine the exercise above with a prescribed activity. For example, picking something up and putting it down in another part of the room, shaking hands and making eye-contact with different members of the group, removing and putting on your shoes.

EXERCISE 35

Title: Me!

Destination: Awareness

Via: Concentration, trust

Time Needed: 15 minutes

Risk: High

Resources: None

Instructions[55]

a. Move in the space maintaining fluidity of movement and flexibility of direction and rhythm.

b. At any point any member of the group may raise their arms in the air and then shout 'Me!' at which point they begin to fall either forwards or backwards with a straight body.

c. Other members of the group have to move quickly to prevent that person falling.

55 This exercise involves a high degree of trust and requires thorough preparation via other concentration, awareness and trust exercises. It is wise to begin the exercise with a smaller group in a confined space while the rest of the group observe. The size of the group and the space can then be increased as awareness and trust are built.

EXERCISE 36

Title: Mirrors

Destination: Physical awareness

Via: Observation, concentration, trust

Time Needed: 15+ minutes

Risk: Low

Resources: None

Instructions

a. Find a partner and decide on who is 'A' and who is 'B'.

b. 'A' and 'B' stand opposite one another looking directly into one another's eyes. 'A' leads an action and 'B' mirrors as accurately and fluidly as possible. There should be no element of competition. Therefore avoid sharp movements that are impossible to follow. Rather try to find a fluid rhythm, with each movement following on naturally from the last. After a period of

69

time and on a given signal from the workshop leader you must swap roles without any break in the movement.

c. The exercise continues as above only this time there is no appointed leader to initiate the action. 'A' and 'B' have to rely solely upon their sense of one another to move as one.

d. Now get into groups of six and face one another in two lines of three. Repeat the exercise without any one person appointed to initiate the action. You must use your peripheral vision to observe the other two members of your line, without turning to face them.[56]

56 Build up this exercise in stages over a period of time. Spot when concentration is flagging and change the activity.

Variation 1

Find a partner and together go through stage b of the exercise above. However, instead of mirroring each other mimetically, this time try enlarging and then reducing the size of your partner's mime as you mirror. In other words imagine that the mirror they are facing is distorted.

EXERCISE 37

Title: The Motorway Game

Destination: Awareness

Via: Co-ordination, observation

Time Needed: 30+ minutes

Risk: Low

Resources: None

Instructions

a. Find a partner and stand opposite one another on different sides of the room. The group as a whole should be in two lines. The space in between these lines represents a motorway.

b. Think of a message to send in mime to your partner on the other side.

c. Next take it in turns to send your message to each other. You may meet up with your partner in the middle of the motorway in between messages to verify that you have understood the message correctly.

Variation 1

As above except that the messages may be sent only using the face or hands.

Variation 2

Each side thinks of a message and when ready sends it simultaneously to the other side.[57]

EXERCISE 38

Title: It Takes What It Takes

Destination: Awareness

Via: Concentration, incorporation

Time Needed: 30+ minutes

Risk: Medium/high

Resources: A song well learned or a short scene well prepared

Instructions[58]

Perform a song either on your own or as a group. At the same time you will be given an extra task to accomplish. For example, calculating a set of mathematical data (such as adding and subtracting numbers), counting the number of lights in a room, building a structure, picking up a series of objects, throwing and catching a ball, drawing something on a piece of paper, feeling the texture and shape of an object.

You must complete the extra task by the end of the song. This must detract as little as possible from the performance of the song itself. You must either incorporate the task within the action of the song or accomplish the task surreptitiously (i.e. at a different level to the performance of the song).

Variation 1

Perform a whole scene whilst undertaking a specific task.

57 The leader needs to establish a time limit in advance of this variation as the messages must be sent in a continuous loop.

58 Whenever you are singing, try to keep your senses open and alive. You will need to incorporate what you see, hear, touch, feel and think into how you shape the text and music. You can do this exercise as a group or divide into smaller groups with some watching while others play. The song you perform can be as simple as a nursery rhyme or be a more technically challenging piece. As always, make sure you are relaxed before starting.

EXERCISE 39

Title: Blind Sculpture

Destination: Physical awareness

Via: Observation

Time Needed: 15+ minutes

Risk: Low

Resources: None

Instructions[59]

59 Exercises that deny the use of sight aim to re-awaken other senses that may have become dulled. This exercise also breaks down physical inhibitions relating to other characters on stage. The tips of the fingers become the eyes.

a. Get into pairs ('A' and 'B'). 'As' stand in a line facing their partner 'B'.

b. 'As' stand still while 'Bs' move forward to stand in front of them. 'Bs' then take two paces back and close their eyes, still facing their partner.

c. 'As' make a sculpture where they are standing with their body.

d. When all the 'As' have made their sculpture, 'Bs' move forward with eyes closed towards their partner who should still be approximately two paces away.

e. 'Bs' use their hands to gain as much information about their partner's physical sculpture as possible including details of the fingers, feet and face.

f. When confident that they have as much information as possible, they take two paces back, eyes still closed, and create their partner's sculpture in a mirror image opposite them.

g. 'Bs' now open their eyes and together the pair make observations as to how identical the sculptures are.

h. 'As' and 'Bs' swap roles and begin again.

IMAGINATION AND SPONTANEITY

Imagination is the capacity to respond (physically and mentally) to stimuli that come from the prompting of one's own internal life. Central to any performance is an act of imagination that transforms the performer into character. It is your imagination that brings a text to life, that supplies the fresh impulse and thought to your action and that enables you to respond to the ideas of other performers, the stage director and the musical director. Furthermore, in theatre you use your imagination to draw upon your inner life experience. This creates an internal energy that you reveal the moment you appear on stage. Imagination is therefore an important building block in the development of stage presence. Using terminology proposed originally by Eugenio Barba, we might refer to the idea of a 'dilated body' and a 'dilated mind' as the physical and mental aspects of stage presence.

It is important to find a connection between the mental and the physical imagination, the thought and the action that arises from it. Your action is the consequence of your thought and therefore they are interdependent.

Spontaneity is about responding to what 'actually' happens rather than what you expected to happen. To develop spontaneity you must train yourself to listen and respond. This training may happen partly through improvisational situations designed to encourage a flexible set of responses by you as character and build upon your observation of life. With respect to characterisation it is vital that you use the rehearsal time to define the music and dramatic ingredients of your role in a very precise way. Clarity at this stage will later enable you to focus all your energy into recreating the role as if discovering each moment for the first time.

EXERCISE 40

Title: Life Story
Destination: Imagination
Via: Spontaneity
Time Needed: 5+ minutes
Risk: Low
Resources: None

Instructions

Find a partner and take two minutes to tell each other your life stories.

60 You can extend the time limit during any version of this exercise. As the time allocated extends you face the challenge of maintaining the energy behind the imaginative process even though your mind might become blank. At this point you must trust that ideas will come and maintain concentration so that the imaginative process is not broken.

Variation 1

Re-tell your life stories in terms of things said, conversations shared, advice taken or descriptions of images remembered.[60]

EXERCISE 41

Title: Creative Visualisation

Destination: Imagination

Via: Mental pictures

Time Needed: 20 minutes

Risk: Low

Resources: Pianist or recording of a piece of music

Instructions

A creative visualisation used in conjunction with a piece of music can be particularly effective in stirring the imagination. The overture to *The Magic Flute* has in the past worked extremely well when used to this effect. The visualisation itself may start with a general relaxation exercise without any music. At the beginning and end of this and other creative visualisation exercises it is important to 'ground' yourself. An example of this technique follows together with a suggested beginning (d) and end (e) to the visualisation with music.[61]

61 The precise text used by the leader during the visualisation will depend solely on the music chosen and the imaginative purpose to which it is put. Above all performers should be allowed to listen to the music, prompted only occasionally by the leader. In this way the music itself will help generate images.

a. Stand comfortably in a quiet place where you won't be disturbed. Relax your body completely. Starting from the toes, and working your way to the scalp, think of relaxing each muscle in your body in turn, letting go of all tension. Breathe deeply and slowly. Close your eyes and count from ten to one, feeling more and more relaxed with each count.

b. As you breathe out imagine that you are putting roots down from the soles of your feet through the floor and way into the earth. Each time you breathe out imagine that these roots are penetrating further and further into the earth.

c. As you breathe in imagine that you are also drawing energy up from the earth, flowing up through your feet and along your spine to all parts of your body.

Practise this until the flow is established concurrently in both directions. It may help to imagine the energy as a white light or the flow of water.

d. Lie down on the floor and make sure that you are comfortable. Imagine that you are looking at yourself in a mirror. Study your face in every detail. When the music begins you will pass through this mirror to a world beyond. Now as you listen to the music you begin to float. Now you are flying high in the sky passing over many different lands. Picture these places in your mind's eye, taking some time to imagine the many details – mountains, forests, deserts, people, whatever suits your fancy.

e. Towards the end of the music you see a clearing towards which you now head slowly, nearer and nearer until very gently you land. Gradually you feel your body in contact with the floor once again in this space. In your own time, open your eyes.

E X E R C I S E   4 2

Title: 10 Objects in the Room

Destination: Imagination

Via: Awareness, concentration

Time Needed: 10 minutes

Risk: Low

Resources: None

Instructions[62]

a. Find a space in the room and spend several silent minutes observing the environment.

b. Close your eyes and answer the leader's questions about the room and the nature of its environment. For example: What colour are the curtains? How many windows are there in the room? Where is the high pitched sound coming from? Members of the group answer at will without opening their eyes.

c. Open your eyes, stand up and then run around the room touching ten different objects and giving each thing a name that it is not. For example, touch the floor and shout the word 'Butter!'.

d. Repeat stages a–c.

Variation 1

As above only use more specific areas of attention. For example, an area through a window or within a circle.[63]

62 The next two exercises have been adapted from two exercises in Keith Johnstone's book *Impro*. The first is designed to make the familiar seem unfamiliar. Although it is primarily a group exercise, there is no reason why you could not undertake a version of it on your own.

63 You can extend or shorten the time limit during any version of this exercise.

EXERCISE 43

Title: The Imagination Game

Destination: Imagination

Via: Spontaneity

Time Needed: 20 minutes

Risk: Medium

Resources: None

64 Say the first word that comes into your head however strange, foolish, rude or inappropriate it may seem.

Much of the time our fear is of saying something that we judge to be too ordinary, too unexciting, too unimaginative. Try therefore to answer any question immediately without censoring your response.

Instructions[64]

a. Sit or stand comfortably in a circle. In response to the leader's commands or questions you must answer or act immediately without pausing for thought. Say the first thing that comes into your head.

b. The leader asks different questions to different members of the group at random.

c. The commands and questions revolve around three main areas:

i   Saying and inventing words. For example: Say a word! Invent a name for a football team, a planet, a colour, a pet octopus etc. The leader may also choose to pursue the names further. For example: Who lives on the planet? What colour is the sky there? What is the principal export of this planet?

ii Miming objects. For example: Take something from the box behind you. What is it? Pass it to the next person. What does it taste of? Pass it on. What is written on it?[65]

iii Creating sounds. Using your voice imitate a piano, a guitar, a trumpet, a drum kit, etc. Next, invent the name of a musical instrument. How is it played? Imitate its sound using your voice. Produce a sound for air, blue, hunger, fear, etc.

65 As above, the leader may begin to pursue a story. Performers should try to make the naming of something coincide with the physical action of finding it. For example, a hand goes to find something and the group member must name it at the moment their hands discover it.

EXERCISE 44

Title: Solo and Ostinato

Destination: Imagination

Via: Improvisation, creating a score, exploring musical textures, characterisation

Time Needed: 20+ minutes

Risk: Medium/high

Resources: Percussion

Instructions[66]

a. As a group, sit in a circle. Each person should have a percussion instrument at the ready. You may wish to use 'body percussion' instead. You are the orchestra whose job it is to make music.

b. Three hand signals will define either 'solo', 'ostinato' (a repeated rhythmic or melodic pattern) or 'drone' (a sustained note). One finger in the air means 'solo'. Two fingers in the air means 'ostinato'. Three fingers in the air means 'drone'.

c. A leader moves to the centre of the circle. It is the job of this leader to act as composer and conductor at the same time. Using the signals, he or she begins by bringing in different members of the orchestra at different times in order to play either an ostinato, a solo or a drone. The composer is seeking to create a musical texture.

d. As the leader you may at any point indicate for someone to stop. Use another sign such as a slicing of the hand across the air. However, this person may be brought back in at any particular point and not necessarily with the same rhythm.

At any point you may give individual instructions to any member of the group or the whole group at once that affect the musical dynamic. For example, louder/softer, faster/slower.

e. At any point the leader may bring the improvisation to an end and hand over to another composer. The new composer may chose to rearrange the players in a different order around the circle or into sections of sound. Alternatively the leader may hand over to another composer during the exercise. Although this saves time and may be less daunting, it is nevertheless less satisfactory as an essential part of the experience revolves around the building up of patterns to support the solo lines.

Variation 1

The exercise proceeds as above only with a vocal section in the 'orchestra'.

66 At its most basic level this exercise frees the imagination. At a more complex level it seeks to apply this to characterisation. As an interpreter, the more a performer relates to the idea of using sound to communicate meaning, the more imaginative their service to the score.

Variation 2

As above with voices only.

Variation 3

The composer is given a task to achieve such as creating a particular environment with the music. For example, seascape, outer space, desert.

Variation 4

Play Exercise 93, 'Dickens', from Chapter 5 and then try recreating a character using music and text.

Variation 5

One half of the group creates an environment while the other half of the group begin an improvised scene that either may or may not take account of the music as it unfolds.

EXERCISE 45

Title: 101 Things to Do with an Object

Destination: Imagination

Via: Improvisation

Time Needed: 15+ minutes

Risk: Low

Resources: A selection of objects

67 This is one of the oldest improvisation games. It aims to give an object an imaginary life that both transforms it and heightens reactions to it.

Instructions[67]

a. Sit in a circle. In the centre of this circle place one or more familiar or unusual objects.

b. Take it in turns to come into the middle and use the object as something other than what it was intended for. Alternatively transform the object into something else by bringing your body into interplay with it.

Variation 1

Play a scene that you have already rehearsed (i.e. not improvised) only this time use the furniture and props from the scene in ways that are different from their original purpose.

Variation 2

A series of objects is needed for this variation. Mark out a stage space in the room with coloured tape. Take it in turns to place the objects in this space. As you do so be aware of the changing nature of this environment. Next stand in the space and imagine a room that is suggested by the arrangement of the objects around you. Observers can ask questions to elicit details about this room, drawing the imagination first by questions about sensory perceptions then by more wide-ranging and detailed investigations.

Variation 3

In this variation begin with an object which you then present to another person with one item of information about that object. This person also has an object which they give to you with one piece of information about their object. Now move on and exchange your new object with someone else. Each time the objects are exchanged you add one piece of information.

E X E R C I S E   4 6

Title: 101 Things to Do with an Action

Destination: Imagination

Via: Improvisation

Time Needed: 15+ minutes

Risk: Low

Resources: None

Instructions

a. Stand comfortably in a circle. One member of the group mimes an action.

b. When this is established the next member of the group along takes over the same action as accurately as possible and then proceeds to change it in some way.

c. The exercise finishes when the action has passed around the circle in this way.[68]

68 Find your ideas through a process of physical discovery *in situ* rather than deciding and then ordering the body. In this exercise the physical action leads the imagination.

79

EXERCISE 47

Title: Musical Sculptures

Destination: Imagination

Via: Listening

Time Needed: 10+ minutes

Risk: Low/medium

Resources: A selection of music either improvised or recorded

Instructions[69]

a. Find a partner. One of you is 'A' and the other 'B'.

b. All the 'As' form a straight line facing opposite the Bs', who are similarly lined up.

c. Using your body (including the face) 'A' forms a sculpture that suggests a feeling, a mood, or an attitude (joy, sadness, thoughtfulness, etc).

d. A piece of music is played. 'B' listens to the music for at least 30 seconds before beginning to manipulate 'A' into a different sculpture. The sculpture that 'B' creates is a direct response to a mood, feeling, or atmosphere stimulated or suggested to you by the music. As a sculptor you must not demonstrate what you want. Rather you must actually mould 'A's body down to the smallest detail.

e. When all the 'Bs' have finished, observe the different responses to the same music and then repeat the exercise with a new piece of music. 'As' and 'Bs' swap places.[70]

Variation 1

In this variation the sculptor doesn't touch the sculpture but makes realistic gestures from a distance as if they were moulding the sculpture. The sculpture must respond to the gestures as if these were causing the sculpture to mould itself.

69 Musical 'appreciation' – listening and commenting on what is heard – develops your ability to hear with greater penetration. For the performer this is only a first step, which eventually leads to an emotional choice in performance. In some performers the emotional response is strong but their attention to what is going on around them may be weak. In others the opposite may be true. Emile Jacques-Dalcroze uses the terms 'inner hearing' and 'outer hearing' to describe the joint responsiveness that you need on stage. The significance of 'inner hearing' is further examined and practised in Chapter 3.

70 Initially, use music where mood or feelings are unambiguous. Film music is a rich source of material. The group members should develop a confidence in forming personal responses that do not strive to be 'correct' but instead honest for them. Gradually introduce music where the mood is more ambiguous or complex. Always encourage the participants to come to a decision.

3 Rhythm, pulse and time

The exercises in this chapter highlight different issues surrounding rhythm, pulse and time. They serve primarily to give rhythm a physical dimension. In addition they involve translating prescribed rhythmic patterns into the internal impulses necessary for autonomic (involuntary) response. We have simplified the music and drama elements so that you need only focus on the area of technique directly relevant to the exercise.

RHYTHM AND TIME

Rhythm, pulse and time are concepts integral to expression in all the performing arts. Rhythm is movement in time. For a musician it becomes a movement of sound. For a lighting designer it becomes a movement of light. For a set and costume designer it becomes a movement of line, texture and colour. As a performer you are aware of all these elements though ultimately you are concerned with the rhythm of an interpretation. You can think of this as a movement of thoughts and feelings translated into character.

When you construct a character, you will do so from the natural rhythms of everyday life (walking, talking, eating, laughing, crying, speaking, thinking, feeling, etc). In sung theatre you have to expand and compress a character's rhythms in order for the drama to function within a musical framework. This is particularly true of the rhythm of your character's thoughts and feelings. The combination of music and text changes our perception of time passing in such a way that time can appear to accelerate, decelerate or even be suspended. For example, this may happen when moving from the speed of thought often necessary in recitative to the more sustained expression of emotion in the aria, or when moving from spoken text to song. Within a dramatic context you can make sense of the rhythms generated by the relationship of music to text by playing with time. You can use this interpretative game to determine when an action, thought or emotion is most effectively and truthfully initiated or completed. This in turn fuels the intention and motivation of your character in action, thought and feeling.

EXERCISE 48

Title: Silent Four

Destination: Awareness of silence

Via: Concentration, relaxation

Time Needed: 10+ minutes

Risk: Low

Resources: Any form of percussion that is loud enough to keep time

1 This exercise can be repeated often. Remember that many of the tensions of everyday life can block the channels of awareness necessary to internalise pulse.

2 As the group becomes accustomed to the pulse, encourage them to feel the beat rests internally.

3 Many of the group members will have relied on watching others to gauge when the silence finishes. Closing the eyes forces each person to take responsibility for feeling the silence. If this stage of the exercise destabilises

Instructions[1]

a. As a group, form a circle.

b. A leader beats time.

c. You must clap in unison for four beats and rest in unison for four beats, clap for four beats and rest for four beats. Repeat this.[2]

d. When the leader ceases to beat out the pulse, you must continue to clap for four beats then rest for four beats. It is important not to shorten the silence.

e. Repeat stages b–d, this time with your eyes closed.[3]

PULSE

In music, silences are called rests and yet 'rest' is the one thing a performer should never do at these moments. Sustaining a character (and implicit within this, an emotion) when not singing is vital. This is difficult partly because it is easy to lose concentration and focus when you are not singing and partly because of the extreme changes in physical energy that take place when you start or stop singing. Furthermore, because music provides its own anchor points you may in performance rely on counting the number of bars until you are next required to sing rather than relating to the dramatic reason why you stopped or are about to start singing. When not singing it may be tempting to count in the head, *with* the head or conduct with other assorted body parts. Any of these are enough to show that you are not in character at that moment. Many of these conscious or unconscious traits are visible and distracting to the audience.

Learn to feel the pulse inside your body rather than externalise it. This will free you mentally and physically to execute real time activities.

EXERCISE 49

Title: In Between

Destination: Feeling a pulse

Via: Group awareness

Time Needed: 5+ minutes

Risk: Low

Resources: None

Instructions

a. Get into two groups of equal numbers ('A' and 'B'). One half stands in a semi-circle opposite the other, with a small gap in between.

b. Group 'A' begins to clap a steady pulse. This can be done with a count-in (1–2–3–4) from a leader within the group.

c. When group 'A' has established its pulse clearly, group 'B' begins to clap the same pulse only this must start exactly in-between the pulse of group 'A'.

d. When group 'B' has established its pulse, group 'A' stops.

e. Group 'A' must wait at least fifteen seconds before restarting its pulse, placing it in-between the pulse of group 'B'.

f. When group 'A' has re-established its pulse then group 'B' stops.

g. Continue as above.[4]

the confidence of the group then repeat stages b–d with eyes open. Remind the group that looking at each other is not helpful in internalising the pulse.

The last stage of the exercise introduces a dilemma particular to making music in groups. If one section of the group comes in earlier than the rest, do you try to keep the ensemble together or do you stick to your guns knowing you are right and that the others are wrong? In rehearsal it is probably better to allow a break in the ensemble, to highlight the mistake. However, there is a point at which this approach will itself begin to destabilise the group dynamic.

4 This game plays with our perception of the pulse. In order to place a pulse between an existing beat we must hear the new pulse relative to the existing one. In this case when group 'B' starts its pulse we hear it as an offbeat within the pulse of group 'A'. However, when group 'A' stops then we begin to hear group 'B' as the main beat. The longer group 'A' is silent before restarting its pulse, the harder it is to perceive the pulse of group 'B' as taking place on an offbeat.

Variation 1

Instead of clapping, stamp with alternate feet to create the beat.

EXERCISE 50

Title: Nursery Rhythm

Destination: Rhythmic awareness

Via: Concentration

Time Needed: 10+ minutes

Risk: Low

Resources: None

5 This exercise aims to build an awareness of each note as vital. The leader may need to beat out the pulse to maintain accuracy. Start slowly.

Instructions[5]

Choose a round that everyone knows (for example, 'London's Burning'). Stand in a circle. Working round the circle each group member sings one syllable of the song. The rhythm of the song must be maintained at all times.

Variation 1

When as a group you are confident with the exercise, introduce the canon. After the second '. . . burning' send the tune round the circle again so that two versions are going round the circle at the same time.

If there are sufficient numbers in the group, try sending a third and fourth version round the circle.

EXERCISE 51

Title: Yes!

Destination: Rhythmic confidence

Via: Observation, concentration

Time Needed: 15+ minutes

Risk: Low

Resources: None

Instructions

a. Stand in a circle. Approximately half the group take off their shoes. These are placed outside the circle.

b. Those people wearing shoes are 'worth' one clap. Those people not wearing shoes are 'worth' two claps. Each clap is worth one beat (one crotchet or quarter-note). Two claps are therefore worth two crotchets (not two quavers or eighth-notes).

c. Everyone starts at the same point in the circle and proceeds in the same direction round the circle, allotting the correct number of claps to each person in turn. In between each person there must be a one beat silence. The discipline of the one-beat silence becomes very important later, so it is important to establish it at this stage.

d. Next repeat the process starting at a different point in the circle and travelling in the opposite direction. When you are ready, move on to the next stage.

e. Several people sit on the floor. These people can be drawn from both those with and without shoes. The people on the floor are 'worth' three claps (three crotchet beats).

f. Repeat stages c–d incorporating the three claps and remembering the one beat silence after each person. When you are ready, move on to the next stage.

g. Divide into two groups ('A' and 'B'). Repeat stages c–d, only this time group 'A' starts at one point in the circle and group 'B' starts at another point. Any two points are possible, though it is simplest for you to start with the first member of your group.

h. Both groups work their way around the whole circle. Here the discipline of the one-beat silence is crucial, as the two groups will not be clapping the same rhythm at the same time. When each group arrives back where it started they shout: 'Yes!'[6]

i. When you are ready, move on by dividing up again this time into four groups. Now each group starts at a different point in the circle.[7]

Variation 1

Play the exercise at different speeds. Introduce points in the circle where the rhythm is louder or softer. For example, those sitting down are 'worth' three beats starting softer and getting louder.

6 The groups should arrive back where they started at the same time since the overall number of beats is the same for both groups, albeit arranged in a different order. You can decide whether or not to observe the one beat silence directly before the shout.

7 It is not essential to clap the rhythms. You can stamp, slap or vocalise them. It is not essential that the pattern is of one, two or three beats, however it is logical to begin with simple ingredients. It is important that everyone understands the rhythmic value of the patterns and that the time between is clear.

EXERCISE 52

Title: Rhythmic Breakdown

Destination: Sense of pulse

Via: Physical representations of rhythm

Time Needed: 10 minutes

Risk: Low

Resources: None

Instructions

Stand in a circle and then beat out the rhythm in Figure 14 (see Appendix). Use your hands to clap (CL) and your feet to stamp (RF = Right Foot, LF = Left Foot).

The following variations also use the rhythm in Figure 14.

Variation 1

Going round the circle each person in turn claps or stamps one note while trying to maintain the rhythm.

Variation 2

Going round the circle each person beats out one crotchet's worth (quarter-note) of the rhythm.

Variation 3

One half of the group starts at bar 1 and the other half at bar 3.

Variation 4

Find a partner and stand opposite them. Each pair starts at the same time although one person starts at bar 1 and the other person at bar 3.

Variation 5

Repeat all the above using Figure 15.

EXERCISE 53

Title: Breakdown and Sustain

Destination: Sustaining physical and vocal energy

Via: Rhythmic precision, improvisation, imagination

Time Needed: 10+ minutes

Risk: Medium/High

Resources: None

Instructions

This exercise is for use with Figures 14, 15, 16, 17. The abbreviation *Sus* denotes a sustained movement whereby you squat down with your back straight. As you do so your arms circle and cross in front of the body. As you stand up, raising yourself up on to your toes, the arms rise extended above the head. Finish up by placing your heels firmly in contact with the floor and allow your arms to complete the circle ready for the next clap as marked in the figures.[8]

Variation 1

As a group line up along the wall. Beat out Figure 16, moving forward across the room as you stomp your feet.

Variation 2

As a group split into two lines of equal numbers, facing one another. Both groups beat out the rhythm but one group starts a bar later than the other.

Variation 3

Line up in three groups across three corners of the room. Each group beats out the rhythm shown in Figure 17, coming in one bar after each other.

Variation 4

Repeat Figure 17 as one group with everyone starting at the same time.[9]

8 Adding a vocal sound to accompany the sustained movement introduces imagination through improvisation. Improvising a vocal sound (as opposed to a pitched note) is always a high-risk activity. Therefore make sure that members of the group are supportive of one other before attempting any vocal improvisation.

9 Do not cut short the sustained movement. Enjoy its energy.

Variation 5

Repeat the above but with a change in dynamics during the vocal sound. For example, loud to soft, soft to loud, a warm timbre to a harsh timbre. Introduce abstract dynamic changes. For example, white to black, joy to sadness, hot to cold.

EXERCISE 54

Title: Heigh-ho

Destination: Co-ordinating a song and an action

Via: Concentration, awareness, singing

Time Needed: 15+ minutes

Risk: Low

Resources: Shoes

10 This exercise is a variant of a work song in which something is passed (in this case shoes) while singing. There are many of these to be found the world over as they arise from the need to unify a group activity involving physical work.

Instructions[10]

For this exercise you will need to know the song 'Heigh-ho' from Disney's *Snow White*. We used to sing a version of this at school using the following words:

> Heigh–ho, heigh-ho, it's off to work we go
> With a bucket and spade and a hand grenade
> Heigh-ho, heigh-ho, heigh-ho
> Heigh-ho, heigh-ho, it's off . . ., etc.

a. Remove one of your shoes and sit as a group on the floor in a tight circle. Place your shoe just in front of you.

b. On the first 'heigh' pick up your shoe. On the following 'ho' place your shoe just in front of the person on your right (i.e. you pass your shoe to the right).

c. On the second 'heigh-ho' the above process is repeated using the new shoe now in front of you.

d. During the next line ('It's off to work we go') pick up the new shoe in front of you on or just before the word 'It's'. Instead of passing the shoe, use the shoe to tap the floor just in front of the person on your right. The 'tap' takes place on the word 'off'. Then tap the floor just in front of you (using the same shoe) on the word 'work' and then finally release the shoe in front of the person on your right on the word 'go'.

e.   On or just before the word 'with', pick up the new shoe in front of you. On the word 'bucket', pass it to the right as before.

f.   On the word 'spade', pick up the new shoe in front of you. On the word 'hand' pass it to the right as before.

g.   On the '-nade' of 'grenade', pick up the new shoe in front of you. On the '-ho' it is placed in front of the person on your right.

h.   For the end of the refrain you repeat the 'tap' movement as outlined in stage e, tapping in front of the person on your right, tapping in front of yourselves and then placing the shoe in front of the person on your right.

i.   At this point the refrain has come around to the beginning again and as a group you repeat the process.

Here is a summary of the routine whereby words in italics indicate simultaneous events:

Heigh-*ho (pass)*, heigh-*ho (pass)*, it's *off (tap to right)* to *work (tap in front)* we *go (pass)*
With a *bucket (pass)* and spade and a *hand (pass)* grenade
Heigh-*ho (pass)*, heigh-*ho (tap to right)*
Heigh-*ho (tap in front)*, heigh-*ho (pass)*[11]

Variation 1

Try the exercise standing up. Hold out your left hand. The shoe is passed from the right into the left hand of the next person. The right hand is used to pass.

Variation 2

Repeat the exercise and then Variation 1 with your eyes shut.

[11] The group is only as strong as its weakest member, since everyone must succeed in completing the action for the exercise to be successful. Therefore patience! Build the exercise slowly to avoid unnecessary frustrations arising within the group.

EXERCISE 55

Title: Take the Rest

Destination: Improvising rhythm

Via: Sense of pulse

Time Needed: 10+ minutes

Risk: Low

Resources: A drum to beat time

Instructions

This exercise follows on from 'Silent Four' and begins with the group in a circle.

a.   A leader establishes the pulse.

b.   As a group clap four equal beats together then each member of the group improvises their own rhythm for four beats. Then as a group clap four beats together then each member of the group improvises four beats.

c.   Continue as above until the leader calls an end to the exercise.[12]

12 You do not need to change the improvisation each time. In fact at first it may be off-putting hearing everyone else's improvisation at once. The discipline of the exercise is to return to the four even beats after the four beats of improvisation. To this end remind the group that the four even beats must always be together. When the group becomes confident with this the leader may stop keeping time.

Variation 1

This variation introduces solo improvisation into the exercise above. Instead of everybody improvising at the same time take it in turns to improvise a four-beat solo. After each solo the whole group claps four even beats.

Variation 2

Use other parts of your body to create rhythm.

Variation 3

Vary the number of counts: three, six and eight to begin with, then five and seven.

Variation 4

Improvise using your voice only, exploring the rhythmic potential of the vocal sounds at different pitches and dynamics.

EXERCISE 56

Title: Jets and Sharks

Destination: Co-ordinating complex rhythms using the whole body

Via: Imagination, co-operation, eye-contact

Time Needed: 20+ minutes

Risk: Medium

Resources: None

Instructions[13]

a. Get into groups of no more than six and no fewer than three.[14]

b. Each group is a gang and must devise a 'code' (a mixture of vocal sounds, claps, stamps, etc) to last exactly eight steady beats.

c. Each group finds a space around the edge of the room.

d. The object of the exercise is for each group to cross to an opposite point in the room via the centre of the room whilst performing their code. Maintain your code as a group at all times, especially when you pass through the other groups crossing the room.[15]

Variation 1

In between each eight beat code add Figure 21. Try creating the harmony within your group. Alternatively each group takes a different harmonic line.

EXERCISE 57

Title: Dancing to the Orchestra

Destination: Musical and physical awareness

Via: Imagination, spontaneity, observation, improvisation

Time Needed: 20+ minutes

Risk: Medium/high

Resources: None

Instructions

a. In this exercise different members of a group have different roles. Six to ten people are needed to form a 'human orchestra'. Two people are needed to be the dancers. The rest of the group observe.

b. The orchestra sits in a group to one side of the space. The first dancer stands facing the orchestra. The second dancer stands with their back to the first dancer. Both dancers should ensure that they have enough room to move comfortably. The rest of the group sit on either side of the space where they can observe the action clearly.

c. The first dancer improvises a series of movements to which

13 Before attempting this game it is wise to have worked through some of the earlier rhythm exercises.

14 An even number of groups makes the game more effective.

15 To help the exercise run smoothly establish the pulse with a count-in. Groups should do their gang code several times from where they are standing before crossing. The leader can give a visual signal to start the crossing.

When you have assimilated these basic ingredients, characterise the movement of your crossing, establishing clear eye-contact with the group directly opposite and, through this eye-contact, the tension of rival gangs. Play the feelings of anger, fear and aggression and express them through the rhythm while maintaining a cool exterior.

91

16 The human orchestra needs to pay attention to the 'dynamics' of the movement for which they are playing (for example, speed, intensity, shape and any implicit emotion). In particular they must work to translate the energy that is being transmitted.

This exercise explores many areas, not least questions arising from who is 'initiating' and who is 'responding'. In translating movement into music the orchestra should be aware that this is primarily an imaginative exercise and there is no right or wrong. Everyone taking part (including those observing) should think about and discuss the exercise. To what extent were the two pieces of movement similar or different? Where did the orchestra most effectively describe the movement? Why? How were the dynamics of movement translated into sound and vice versa? Did the orchestra act as an ensemble or as a collection of soloists? Did the orchestra respond primarily to what they saw or what they imagined the 'dancer' felt?

the orchestra improvises an accompaniment. This improvised accompaniment can be a combination of vocal sound and percussive rhythm. It must, however, reflect the dynamic energies of the movement and for this reason the orchestra must watch very closely.

d. The second dancer listens for a while and then begins to improvise a series of movements. These movements are stimulated by the musical accompaniment.

e. The rest of the group must compare and contrast the two pieces of movement.[16]

Variation 1

Try the exercise again with the proviso that the orchestra should focus less on describing the patterns of movement and more on expressing their own internal response to the feeling of the movement or what they believe the emotions implicit in the movement to be. In other words, in the first version the orchestra responds to a stimulus within the dancer but in the second version they respond to a stimulus within themselves (albeit initially provoked by the movement).

EXERCISE 58

Title: Think Again

Destination: Changing the speed of an activity

Via: Imagination

Time Needed: 15+ minutes

Risk: Medium

Resources: None

Instructions

Take it in turns to walk from one end of the room to the other. Walk at a normal pace until you reach the middle. On reaching the middle, however, you must change speed, moving either faster or slower.

You have to invent a reason for the change in speed. For example, an imaginary obstacle, an imaginary situation, a response to a thought that comes to mind.

Variation 1

Repeat the above incorporating two changes of speed.

Variation 2

Repeat the above incorporating a change of direction.[17]

EXERCISE 59

Title: Exaggerating Rhythm

Destination: Exploring a character's rhythm

Via: Awareness, observation

Time Needed: 15 minutes

Risk: Low

Resources: None

Instructions[18]

a. Find a partner at random.

b. Set off across the room with your partner at a steady walking pace with one person following the other person trying to imitate their walk as accurately as possible.

c. Each time the leader calls out a number from one to ten, the person following must exaggerate their imitation by a certain amount. One represents only a slight exaggeration and ten represents a huge exaggeration.

d. Each time the leader claps their hands, the person following must swap positions with the person imitating. In this way the roles are reversed.

18 This exercise looks at the everyday rhythm of walking and involves observing, reproducing and exaggerating someone else's walk. Play it as an introduction to the next exercise, 'Rhythm of Life'.

EXERCISE 60

Title: Rhythm of Life

Destination: Exploring a character's rhythm

Via: Awareness, observation

Time Needed: 30+ minutes

Risk: Medium

Resources: Pencils and paper

19 This exercise looks at rhythm as expressed through everyday behaviour. It involves reproducing someone else's rhythm as a way of challenging your own (possibly unconscious) habits. Everyone has different personal rhythms, from the involuntary rhythms of the heartbeat, breathing and blinking to the rhythms of walking, talking, eating, making love and listening.

20 The choice of activity is wholly dependent upon the rhythm one wishes to explore. For example, if you want to explore the rhythm of speech and the rhythm of listening then you might simply ask the group to sit and have coffee and a chat. If you want to explore the rhythm of movement you might ask members of the group to walk around the space.

21 Towards the end of this exercise increase in scale what you are doing (i.e. exaggerate the rhythm disproportionately). This may help certain elements become clearer to those observing.
   Use this exercise in conjunction with those in Chapter 5. As a study of human

Instructions[19]

a. Find a partner.

b. One of you moves to the side of the room and maintains a position from which you can always see and hear your partner clearly.

c. The other undertakes a series of activities in the space as directed by a leader.[20]

d. Whatever activity is chosen, as an observer you have to make detailed notes (sketches, words or kinesthetic impressions) regarding your partner's rhythm. For example: How slow or fast are they walking? How often do they change direction? What exactly are the mechanics of their walk? Where do they place their energy as they move? Do they have any particular mannerisms?

e. At the end of a period of time determined by the leader, swap roles with your partner and repeat steps b–d.

f. Next, go away with the notes you have taken and try to reproduce your partner's rhythm within yourself as precisely as possible. As part of this process it may be helpful to exaggerate the rhythm disproportionately as a way of assimilating it into your body.

g. At the end of a period of time determined by the leader, take it in turns with your partner to repeat the activity in step c only this time do it as if you were your partner (i.e. with your partner's rhythm).[21]

MUSICAL STRUCTURE

In sung theatre, action, thought and emotion tend to move towards and develop from a moment within the musical structure. In order to find freedom within the formalised structure of music, you must have a thorough knowledge of the score. This knowledge should derive from a physical as well as a mental memory of the music such that it can be executed as if through an involuntary response. In performance this allows you to govern your responses not through a conscious act of will on the singing mechanism but as if through a spontaneous response to the situation in which your character finds him or herself.

   In order to translate our changing perception of time into spatial and emotional terms, you have to harness the creative power of your imagination. It is the imagination that supplies the fresh impulse and thought to action whenever necessary. This enables you to alter the time taken to execute an activity so that the timing of stage action fits or accords with the time suggested by the music. Additional factors, such as the size of the stage and the relative positioning of furniture and props, will affect your timing. However, your imagination will never be free to contribute effectively unless you are comfortable with the mechanics of musical time. For this reason you should be able to:

1 Subdivide the musical pulse into the necessary fractional units, working out the time value of one note relative to the next; then form these units into rhythmic patterns. Crucial to this process is your awareness of any silences and pauses that either form part of a rhythmic pattern or separate one pattern from the next.
2 Translate these patterns into the muscular activity required to sing. This creates physical sensations that will inform a character's emotion, particularly in moments where the energy behind a character's expression changes.
3 Integrate the exterior and interior impulses that generate real time events and musical events so that, at the moment of performance, music, text and action are created from the same spontaneous impulse. Once again, crucial to this process is an understanding that silence is a dynamic part of rhythm involving moments of energy transition or suspension.

Many of the difficulties encountered in the area of rhythm and time arise ultimately from the way in which we learn music. The mathematical ratios used to notate music allow us to reproduce and reinterpret it from a printed score. Learning a piece of music from a score forces you to engage initially on a mathematical level. Subdividing beats in order to work out where notes fall within a given beat is often a performer's first port of call when attempting to understand rhythmic patterns. However, a performer's sense of rhythm is rarely improved using mathematics. Solutions to rhythmic problems that detach you from the feelings implicit within the patterns may solve one problem only to exacerbate another. This is because rhythm is not primarily intellectual but rather physical. It must be felt and sensed rather than counted. If you engage rhythmically in a physical and emotional way then

behaviour it will raise questions regarding character. This is particularly the case when the rhythm is exaggerated or diminished. As the exercise moves away from the art of imitation towards the art of stylisation, a new character seems to emerge.

your power to sustain the emotional life of a character on stage (and consequently characterisation itself) will increase.

EXERCISE 61

Title: Stop and Go

Destination: Internalising pulse

Via: Awareness, concentration

Time Needed: 5+ minutes

Risk: Low

Resources: A drum to beat time

22 Walking in time without an external pulse is comparatively easy. However, freezing for eight counts requires the participants to have a memory of the beat. Maintain your frozen position without showing any external signs of keeping time. It follows that as a group you must also move off together. Furthermore, you must maintain the energy in your body when frozen so that it is sustained ready for release. In this way the freezing becomes an activity in itself. The exercises at the end of Chapter 3 look in more detail at the idea of sustaining energy.

Instructions

a. A leader beats time.

b. Walk in time with the pulse for eight beats then 'freeze' for eight beats. The freeze has to happen exactly on beat 1. After the freeze you must move on the next beat 1.

c. As you become confident with this, the leader will gradually stop keeping time, for example, beating only on beats 1, 3, 5 and 7.[22]

EXERCISE 62

Title: Wander

Destination: Internalising pulse

Via: Spatial awareness, concentration

Time Needed: 10 minutes

Risk: Low

Resources: A drum to beat time

23 This exercise follows on directly from 'Stop and Go'.

Instructions[23]

a. A leader beats time.

b. Walk naturally for eight beats (not consciously in time) and then 'freeze' for eight beats.

c. As you become confident with this the leader will gradually stop beating time. The walking and the stopping must still last the equivalent of eight beats.[24]

Variation 1

Incorporate an eight beat breathing count into the exercise.

• Breathing in over four beats and out over the following four.
• Breathing in over two beats and out over the following six.
• Breathing in over one beat and out over the following seven.[25]

Variation 2

Vary the count from eight beats to six, seven or nine.

Variation 3

Incorporate a song into the above exercise and variations. The song must continue even though the movement has to stop every eight counts. The pulse of the song needs to be the same as the pulse of the beats.

E X E R C I S E   6 3

Title: Magnify

Destination: Awareness of time passing

Via: Imagination

Time Needed: 15+ minutes

Risk: Low

Resources: A drum to beat time

Instructions[26]

a. Take an episode from everyday life, for example, buying a newspaper while waiting for a train. Devise a series of physical actions that last for exactly sixteen beats and which convey this episode. The speed of the beat is determined by a leader. Make sure that you can repeat the actions identically (i.e. the activity must be learned).

b. Now take five minutes to incorporate a change of speed into the same activity. It is up to you to decide on the reason for the change in speed. For example, you thought you had twenty

24 Unlike the previous exercise where the walking provided an external 'anchor' for remembering the beat, here the group must remember the pulse internally, whether they are walking or still.

25 The performer in sung theatre uses the breath differently to the performer in spoken theatre. The demands of musical line and phrasing are such that the surprise or unexpected breath so useful to the actor in re-inventing thought or emotion is less available. Therefore you must re-invent your thought while sustaining breath control.

26 Changing the speed of an action often changes its size and intensity. Changing the intensity of an activity will probably affect its speed and size.

97

minutes before the departure of the train but in fact the doors are already closing.[27]

c.   Now perform your new activity within a count of sixteen beats. Obviously the new activity will be either quicker or slower than the original. However, you must compensate for the change in speed by making sure that the episode still lasts sixteen beats. This compensation must take place without losing any detail in the series of actions. Therefore you must not cut anything from your sequence of actions but must vary the speed at another point in the activity. This in turn may alter the thought process of the character performing the activity. Using the example above where the character realises that he or she must hurry to meet the train (i.e. the action speeds up), the character may saunter more casually up to the newspaper stand as if he or she had all the time in the world (i.e. this portion of the activity slows down to compensate for the speeding up later on).

27 During this period the leader does not need to keep time.

EXERCISE 64

Title: Pick a Spot

Destination: Internalising pulse

Via: Imagination, spatial awareness

Time Needed: 10 minutes

Risk: Low

Resources: A drum to beat time

Instructions

a.   A leader beats time.

b.   Remain still for eight beats. During this time think of a point in the room. For example, a point on the wall or a piece of furniture such as a chair or a mirror.

c.   During the next eight beats fix your eyes on the spot you have chosen and move towards it. When you arrive at your chosen point, touch it exactly on the first beat of the next eight. Therefore you have to judge the speed at which you move so as not to arrive too soon or too late.

d.   Now freeze and in your mind's eye see another point in the room. After eight beats move off again towards the new point.

e.   Repeat stages a–d.

This exercise builds on previous exercises as spatial awareness is incorporated into the movement. You need to pay particular attention to the dynamics of movement. The predetermined nature of musical time can manipulate or control the dynamics of an action or succession of actions in such a way that what you are about to do becomes predictable. If spectators perceive what the performer is about to do then their attention will diminish. The fact that they may already be familiar with the music and text makes it all the more important for you to surprise through each action. There are many ways of achieving this form of dissociation (see Chapter 2) at a technical level. The following are some physical suggestions to try out where appropriate during the following exercises:

1 Instead of continuing in one direction, change course either randomly or in response to a stimulus other than that of the music (for example, a thought, an obstacle or the actions of another character).
2 Begin an action with a part of the body in the opposite direction to that in which the action will finally be directed; in the same way that before throwing a punch the arm is drawn back in the opposite direction.
3 Experiment with slowing an action down and speeding it up.
4 Initiate an action the moment before the rhythm begins and complete it a moment after the rhythm ends.
5 Play with creating a different balance within the body. This will involve altering your normal balance in some way. For example, walking on the sides of your feet, sliding your heels on the floor, moving on tiptoes, with knees slightly bent or moving with a different centre of energy (see Chapter 5).

Variation 1

Repeat the exercise above only this time your objective is to disguise your ultimate destination as pictured in the mind's eye for as long as possible while making sure that you reach your destination at the necessary moment. Therefore you will no longer fix your eyes on the spot chosen but rather experiment with changing direction and moving away from the point imagined before then moving towards it.

You must keep your chosen point in your mind's eye without letting this show in your eye focus until the last possible moment.

Variation 2

Introduce the idea of motivation to the exercise (i.e. a reason why you need to get to a particular point). For example, if the point chosen is a chair then the contact made with the chair could be to check that it is secure enough to sit on.

Variation 3

Experiment with introducing imaginative situations into the exercise. For example, divide the room into zones with different surfaces (slippery, sticky, muddy, painful, etc).

Variation 4

Imagine that the point you are moving towards is an imaginary object. In moving across the space you should be aware of why you are moving towards this object and in touching the object on the precise beat you must reveal your attitude towards that object. You may of course use any part of your body to make contact with the object.

Variation 5

Incorporate a breathing count of eight beats into the above exercise and variations:

- Inhaling over four beats, exhaling over four beats.
- Inhaling over two beats, exhaling over six beats.
- Inhaling over one beat, exhaling over seven.

Variation 6

Incorporate an emotional count into Variation 5 such that when you inhale you are experiencing an inner feeling that increases in scale. For example, you desire to possess the object in question. Instead of exhaling, sustain the breath and with it the emotion. You must nevertheless keep the emotion alive inside over the necessary counts. Exhale and release the emotion when you touch the object.[28]

28 The sustaining of breath must not lead to unwanted physical tension, especially around the chest and shoulders. Supporting your breath will prevent this.

SUSTAINING A MOMENT

Rhythmic ability is only partly about accuracy and precision of execution. It is ultimately about letting go, enjoying the flow of energy that links note to note, pattern to pattern, phrase to phrase. This flow of energy and your power to sustain it relies firstly upon your knowledge of the music and text and secondly on decisions you have made regarding your interpretation (see Chapter 4). Without a flow of energy music and drama will lack line and direction. Sustaining the energy for this line and direction is made more difficult when music seems to decelerate the passage of dramatic events as they would occur in real time.

The following exercises explore the sensation of sustaining energy in your body. You can apply this technique to any situation in which you are called upon to sustain a moment of drama on stage. It is particularly useful for exploiting those moments when you must find a still presence on stage as the music takes on the primary function of creating the scene but where the drama must not stop. This can happen during passages of coloratura, passages where the text repeats, where the passage of text is slow (i.e. where the note values are very long) or during musical interludes. Suspending a moment when music plays with our perception of time may seem to imply putting something on hold. In fact your energy should, at every moment of the suspension, be alive and pulsating.

E X E R C I S E   6 5

Title: Swing!

Destination: Sustaining energy

Via: Physical awareness

Time Needed: 5+ minutes

Risk: Low

Resources: None

Instructions[29]

a. Swing your left arm, feeling its weight.

b. Swing your right arm, feeling its weight.

c. Repeat stages a–b this time sensing the moment of suspension as your arm reaches its highest point both in front of and behind your body. Enjoy the feeling of the potential energy available to you at these moments.

At first only maintain the moment of suspension for as long as it feels natural. As you repeat the exercise, fill these moments with

29 A simple physical activity to encourage a feeling of sustained energy in the body. It is important at such moments to sustain the energy truthfully however easy it is to fake pleasure at the moment of suspension.

an honest pleasure. On each repetition your pleasure increases. In this way the moment suspended becomes longer (sustained). Only if your pleasure is honest will you avoid tension as the moment expands.

d.   Now swing both your arms alternately.

Variation 1

Substitute different feelings for the sensation of pleasure. For example, despair. Whatever feeling you choose the suspension must be a celebration of that feeling.

EXERCISE 66

Title: The Bird

Destination: Sustaining energy

Via: Physical awareness

Time Needed: 10+ minutes

Risk: Low

Resources: None

30 This activity is used as a warm-up by skiers and adapted to suit our purposes. The object is to feel the sustained energy available behind the suspension at certain points in the activity (designated by an asterisk *) and to remember this feeling. The routine is broken down into parts as described and illustrated for the sake of clarity only. When practised it must flow as one fluid movement that can be repeated several times.

Instructions[30]

a.   Begin standing comfortably with your arms by your side (Illustration 1. i).

b.   Your arms then circle backwards (Illustration 1. ii) and when they reach the highest point (i.e. are raised as high as possible above your head), you should also be standing on tip toes (*) (Illustration 1. iii).

c.   Your arms fall forward, sweeping round in a circle as your knees bend slightly and your feet connect again with the ground (Illustration 1. iv and 1. v).

d.   As your arms complete the circle they return momentarily to the position described in step b (*) (Illustration 1.vi). They then fall forward once again only this time you drop down and end up in a crouched position with your arms out behind and head raised (*) (Illustrations 1. vii and 1. viii).

e.   Now reverse the move with your arms sweeping round in a circle in the other direction (Illustration 1. ix and 1. x) and then return to the first position (*) (Illustration 1. xi).

Illustration 1: The Bird

1.i

1.ii

1.iii

1.iv

1.v

1.vi

1.vii

1.viii

1.ix

1.x

1.xi

1.xii

f. Repeat this movement several times. Each time try increasing your sense of pleasure at the feeling of possible energy (*). After the final repetition, return to your initial position with arms by your side and feet firmly on the ground (Illustration xii).

Variation 1

As your arms swing past your feet in step d and reach their furthest point behind you then do a little jump into the air.

Variation 2

Substitute different feelings for the sensation of pleasure. For example, despair. Whatever feeling you choose the suspension must be a celebration of that feeling.

EXERCISE 67

Title: Transfer

Destination: Sustaining a moment

Via: Physical awareness, imagination

Time Needed: 10+ minutes

Risk: Low

Resources: One juggling ball (or other soft ball) per pair

31 This exercise should build on skills developed in the ball throwing exercises outlined in Chapter 2.

Instructions[31]

a. Find a partner and make sure that you have one ball between you.

b. Throw the ball to one another as you move around the space.

c. Whenever you catch the ball, you should allow its energy to travel in your hand along the same axis it would have travelled had you not caught it. You must return the ball and in doing so discover the moment of suspension where the energy of the ball thrown is translated into the energy of the ball thrown back.

You should therefore never block the energy of the ball when you catch it.

EXERCISE 68

Title: The Faraway Hill

Destination: Sustaining an emotion

Via: Physical awareness

Time Needed: 15+ minutes

Risk: Medium/high

Resources: None

Instructions

a.   Get into groups of three.

b.   One person from each group takes their place in a line facing the rest of their group. Each person in the line should have enough room to swing their arms.

c.   The leader says, '1–2–3–throw.' On each of the three counts each person in the line mimes swinging an imaginary ball in their hands to and fro until finally it is released on 'throw'.

d.   As this ball is released then the person throwing must follow its imaginary trajectory with the line of their body and especially with their eyes. The feeling of suspension or sustained energy should increase the further the ball travels. The ball must remain in the air for as long as possible. In other words until the thrower can maintain the energy no longer due to a lapse in concentration, unnecessary physical tension or when the imagination is no longer able to maintain it. Therefore the ball must travel miles and miles and even when it has dipped below the hill on the horizon the person throwing must make us believe that the energy of the ball is still alive.

e.   When the ball finally hits the ground the thrower releases the suspension.

f.   During this the other two members of each group are watching their colleague to see if they believe that the ball is still in the air. If they lose faith in the imaginary ball because suspension has been lost or can no longer be sensed then they raise their hands in the air. The thrower must immediately redouble his or her efforts and then repeat the exercise.

g.   Each member of the group takes it in turn to do the exercise as described above.

h.   The leader may then introduce set periods of time (counts) during which the ball must remain in the air.

i. Eventually you can drop the physical representation of throwing the imaginary ball (i.e. the mime) and play the exercise with the thought or memory of the ball only.

Variation 1

This should follow on from the exercise above once you have assimilated the principles. In this variation the thrower of the ball produces a sound as they throw the ball. The thrower must show the path of the ball with the voice. The same principles apply to this sound as to the body.[32]

Variation 2

This variation can work with both the basic exercise and Variation 1. During the swing of the imaginary ball the thrower recalls an emotion (see Chapter 5) and then releases this emotion with the ball. The same principles apply to this emotion as to the body and voice.[33]

Practise doing the exercise in one controlled breath. As the ball hits the ground so the remaining breath (and emotion) is released.

Practise doing the exercise in two breaths where the intake of the second breath does not break the suspension. Once again it is important to avoid any unnecessary physical tension especially in the shoulders, chest and facial mask.

E X E R C I S E   6 9

Title: Omelette

Destination: Unifying a real time activity with a musical activity

Via: Singing, improvisation, internalising the pulse, sustaining a moment

Time Needed: 25 minutes

Risk: Medium/high

Resources: A piano

Instructions[34]

a.   Learn the song in Figure 25. You must know it absolutely from memory before proceeding.

32 The voice must express the trajectory of the ball and not sound like a note sung. The other group members have the difficult task of sensing whether this is true.

33 Think about your breathing during this exercise. Breath is a means by which thought and emotion can be kept alive. In sung theatre, by maintaining the breath a little longer than the last note one can help sustain the emotion right up until the last moment before a change or reaffirming of thought or emotion becomes necessary. Bear in mind that the way a character breathes will contribute to how the thought or emotion itself is experienced by the audience.

34 This exercise is the culmination of many of the preceding exercises in this chapter. It requires you to internalise the prescribed rhythm to such an extent that you are free to improvise speech and stage action while also carrying out specific musical activities at specific moments.

b. The aim of the exercise is to demonstrate how to make an omelette. The text and music that you have learned are fixed fragments within an improvisation. You must improvise speech and stage action in between the fixed fragments. This improvisation must make sense of the fixed text. The fixed text and music must happen at exactly the right moment as detailed in the score (Figure 25).[35]

Variation 1

As a step towards characterising the scene, introduce variations in situation. For example, you are a participant in a television game show struggling to make an omelette for the first time; you are a very bullish chef giving orders to the latest assignment of catering students; you are a very sophisticated chef famed for your omelettes; you are a rather enthusiastic product demonstrator working on a cruise liner in rough seas.

USING RHYTHM AND PULSE TO CREATE EMOTION

You can use rhythm and pulse as a vehicle for your character's emotion and as a means to create the expressive tensions that give rise to emotion. By distorting rhythm or pulse you can create a tension between what we (the audience) expect and what we actually hear. In rhythm this is done by 'placing' a note fractionally later or earlier than what would be considered mathematically correct. Some musicians describe this as playing on the front of the beat or the back of it. Choosing which note to place is a matter of personal interpretation. It may be your response to the melody, a beautiful note that contrasts with the previous note. It may be your response to the harmony, a chord that moves you. It could be a response to an orchestral accompaniment or the composer's choice of instruments that create a particular sonority. Whatever the stimulus, placing a note will give emphasis, stress or significance to a particular moment. Because it plays with the listener's expectation, you can use it to create surprise and the impression of spontaneity.

In song, when you place a note you inevitably place the word that belongs to it. This, of course, will give stress, emphasis and significance to that word. Deciding where to place a word is not simply a response to the text but to the combination of word and

35 It may be useful for the leader to give a count of four before starting the accompaniment.

This exercise is fiendishly difficult. Initially, allow everyone in the group to practise it at the same time. Later play the game in smaller groups with others observing. Repeat several times before encouraging feedback.

Questions for discussion include: How easy was it to maintain precision in the moments of fixed music and text? How did the pressure of improvising within a fixed time affect the improvisation? In the course of repeating the exercise did you discover any techniques that made the exercise easier?

music. Therefore your choice could be stimulated by the combination of a word within a particular melody, or the harmony that accompanies a word, or indeed the sound of the particular instrument used to accompany a word. It follows that you can distort the rhythm to create surprise and spontaneity within the text as well as within the music. In other words, distorting the rhythm is a response to both the music (including the accompaniment) and the words.

In sung theatre you will distort the rhythm not just in response to the music and the words but also in response to the dramatic context. It becomes an expression of your action and reaction, revealing nuances of your character's attitude to their situation and environment. This includes your awareness of the physical and emotional energy of other characters. That one character on stage should be aware of the presence and energy of another is perhaps obvious, but that this awareness can and should be revealed through the nuances of rhythm is less obvious. It requires co-ordination and surety of rhythm and awareness.

If you are sufficiently confident in your sense of rhythm you will remain open to the influence of the music, text and dramatic context which must necessarily play upon the precise execution of rhythms.

Distorting or playing with the pulse is known in music as *rubato* (literally 'stolen'). This idea of stealing time is used to convey the sense of give and take within the musical pulse, as if the pulse contains an elasticity that allows it to be stretched and compressed. In performance *rubato* creates a tension between what we (the audience) perceive the precise pulse should be and what we actually hear. The speeding up and slowing down of the music is a means by which you can both stimulate emotion within the audience and translate your own emotional impulses into musical interpretation. In sung theatre the performer's emotional impulses are necessarily replaced by their character's emotional impulses. Distorting the pulse arises from a response to exactly the same stimuli as those that influence the precise execution of rhythms. However, whereas placing a note or word is a momentary event, *rubato* exists over a length of time and requires what is 'stolen' to be 'paid back'. If the pay-back does not happen, then the music has merely slowed down or speeded up. Ideally the amount of real time needed for a passage remains the same whether or not *rubato* is used. This means that whenever the pulse is stretched it must then be compressed. Where the accompaniment follows the *rubato* of the melody then all involved (i.e. soloists and conductor) must maintain an internal sense of where the precise beat would fall if they were to execute the music in strict tempo. If you are not aware of this internal sense of pulse, then you are less open to exploit the emotional potential that arises from the tension between the two. Internalising the pulse also allows you to practise a dissociation of real time and musical time. The ability to do this can free you to explore the expressive tensions between real time stage action and music.

There are no fixed rules as to when and how one places notes or uses *rubato*. There are, however, considerations, in particular the musical tastes of those involved and their different understandings of musical style and idiom. Clearly you are more free to effect *rubato* in a solo than you are singing as part of an ensemble. In theory you do not need to decide beforehand exactly where you want to place a note or play with the pulse. Each performance should be fresh and there will hopefully be changes of nuance in each. However, rehearsal will inevitably involve the exploration of musical and dramatic ideas during which you will need to incorporate the vision of the stage director and musical director. Therefore many moments of 'give and take' will be established in rehearsal.

A further exploration of the relationship between text and music takes place in the following chapter.

4 Music, text and the score

This chapter explores the relationship between music and text as found in a vocal score. Action, character, situation and emotion are also component parts of this relationship and as such will inevitably feature in this chapter. However, they are dealt with more fully in the next chapter. The exercises here are designed to offer approaches to unlocking the music and text so that interpretative choices present themselves more easily, giving you greater flexibility and control during the rehearsal process.

Where appropriate you should feel free to experiment with colouring your vocal sound in a myriad possible ways. For example, relaxed, intense, loud, soft, high, low, legato, staccato, sweet, steely, breathy, etc. Some of the exercises make use of nonsense sounds in order to facilitate this. Generally speaking the use of nonsense is designed to free you up from the pressures of having to make sense and thereby to release your imagination through sound.

Some exercises require you to make a choice about the text that you are going to use. This can be a text that you have not encountered before, a text you have chosen to work on over an extended period or one that you are preparing for performance. A number of exercises require a sung text known to the group as a whole. In all cases the exercises will help generate a freshness towards using and hearing language.

Before commencing any work on the interpretation of text, it is worth stating that many problems arise from a simple lack of clarity in diction. There is no substitute for engaged vowels and highly energised consonants. Figures 22, 23 and 24 are further examples of warm-up exercises you can use to practise this. You may find articulation exercises useful in that they propel the tongue, teeth and lips to move more quickly, which in turn helps make the language more active. However, such exercises must be combined with others if the overall use of words is to be enhanced.

We have chosen not to give a suggested time for the following exercises as this really does depend on each individual or group. If an exercise goes on too long then the use of words can rapidly become meaningless and the exercise tedious.

APPROACHING THE SCORE

In spoken theatre it is not uncommon for an actor to delay learning text until the rehearsal process itself. In doing so he or she is trying to remain open to possibilities in interpretation arising from the rehearsal process – in particular from the influence of the stage director and the ideas of other performers in character.

In sung theatre the situation is more complex. Specific technical challenges arise from the extra-daily muscular activity involved in singing. The more challenging a role is vocally, the more important it is for you to familiarise yourself with the precise muscular activity necessary to sing the role. Technical challenges specific to voice production are usually resolved before detailed work on interpreting text and character begins. The music (including pitch, rhythm, dynamics, colour and stylistic nuance) and the text (in particular the formation of vowels and the articulation of consonants) are central to this familiarisation. Singing a role into the voice, as this process is referred to, inevitably leads to learning.

There are a number of issues here, keenly felt by performer, stage director and musical director alike. You may find that in learning the score prior to rehearsals, you consciously or unconsciously make interpretative decisions which you later find do not coincide with the vision of the stage director and musical director. Furthermore, the choices you make may not coincide with interpretations that other performers have brought to the rehearsal room. In accommodating the wishes of the stage director and musical director, who between them are responsible for the overall coherence of the production, new technical difficulties inevitably surface. Ideally at this stage a performer requires the time and space to sing new ideas into the voice. If you sense that this time is not available then you are more likely to resist these ideas.

If, in an attempt to be more open to other ideas, you learn the score less well prior to rehearsals, you may find that you do not have sufficient time to deal with the many different demands being made of you by composer, librettist, musical director, stage director and choreographer. What is more, many technical challenges in voice production may not become apparent until you fully engage emotionally in what you are singing.

In an ideal world you would have the time and facility to make all the necessary adjustments, both technical and interpretative, during the rehearsal process. The reality is that there is often insufficient time. In approaching a score you are faced with choices. The greater the number of possibilities you are able to explore prior to rehearsal as part of the learning process, the more flexible you will be in rehearsal. However, this is not as simple to achieve in practice as it is to state in theory.

LEARNING THE SCORE

As we have said, the process of memorising involves learning the score in such a way that the totality of text and sound is absorbed into the muscle memory. In addition to the work you will do on your own, you may also call upon the services of the singing teacher, the singing coach, the language coach or the repetiteur (rehearsal pianist). The singing teacher is concerned primarily with the technique of voice production. The singing coach is concerned primarily with using technique in conjunction with imagination to develop an interpretation while you are learning a role. The language coach is concerned primarily with correct techniques of pronunciation when singing in a foreign language. A repetiteur may be useful at any stage of the learning process to ensure that you are learning the score accurately or as an accompanist as you sing through the material. Some or all of these roles may overlap.

There is no one way to learn a score as inevitably each person will respond to the many challenges in different ways and with different strengths. You may find the following observations helpful:

1 The process of learning cannot really begin without a thorough knowledge of the story (context) to be gained by reading the text

or libretto in its entirety. Reading a synopsis is also helpful, but not sufficient.

2 You can accelerate the process of memorising the text, and consequently the music, by writing your character's words out in full (including the interjections of other characters).

3 In asking a repetiteur to make a recording, bear in mind that there are several possibilities:

- To record the text, accompaniment and vocal line.
- The text and vocal line without the accompaniment (i.e. doubling the vocal line on the piano).
- The accompaniment without text or vocal line.
- The vocal line without text or accompaniment.
- Variations of the above incorporating the text and vocal lines of other characters.

Each of these possibilities will help you in a specific way, depending on how advanced you are in your learning. For instance, if you are having difficulty pitching accurately the intervals between notes it is of more use to record the vocal line alone. If the repetiteur feels that the harmony within the accompaniment helps this process then he or she should record the vocal line with the accompaniment. If you are secure with your own text and vocal line then it is more useful to record only the accompaniment and the lines of other characters.

4 If you find it helpful to listen to recordings then listen to as many interpretations of your role as possible. Listening to recordings will not only give an idea of some of the possible choices open to you but will also provide essential information as to the role of the orchestra in the telling of the story. Recordings are only useful as background research to your own interpretation.

5 When learning vocal material in a foreign language, bear in mind that this involves more than just knowing how to pronounce words and vowel sounds accurately. It requires a literal translation as well as an understanding of the meaning that underlines this translation, including references and connotations. The learning process must lead eventually to a connection between you and the text. This can only happen when the meaning of the text you are singing is absolutely second nature. This in turn will free you to effect nuances of interpretation through changes in stress and inflection that nevertheless remain appropriate for that language.

6 Familiarising yourself with the other vocal parts and the accompaniment (aural awareness) is a vital stage in the learning of musical entries as this can be more easily integrated into the life of a character on stage than simply counting bars rest in the head.

Finally, memorising inevitably involves repetition or learning by rote. Effective memory work leads naturally to the singing of text and music as if through an involuntary response. There is a pitfall here. Excessive repetition by rote can also lead to a loss of spontaneity. This is precisely because the response has become automatic. You must therefore be aware that this involuntary execution of sung material is only the blank canvas upon which you paint an interpretation. In order for interpretation to be truly free you must almost forget that you know the material, always finding within you the thought and feeling that leads to expression.

Learning can easily become stale and mechanised. Use the exercises in this chapter in conjunction with your memorising work to reawaken your desire to learn.

INTERPRETING THE SCORE

Interpreting a score is a journey of revelation. On this journey you will initially be concerned with the discovery of signposts. These are contained within moments of musical tension, within the text and within the way in which the two come together. They are indicated in many possible ways. For example:

- The choice of cadence at the end of a phrase.
- A harmonic sequence.
- A change in speed.
- A change in dynamics.
- The interval between two notes.
- A change of key.
- Changes in rhythmic patterns.
- Changes of harmony.
- Silences.
- Characterising agents such as accent, staccato and fermata.
- The substance of words (in particular the length of vowels and the quality of consonants).
- Significant word choices.

- The use of rhyme.
- The use of imagery.
- The style of text (formal, poetic, naturalistic, surreal, etc).
- Linguistic devices such as antitheses and oxymoron.
- Non-verbal sounds as well as the content of the text itself.

You must ultimately translate these signposts into a character's behaviour. You will communicate your interpretation through the dramatic subtext that suggests what your character is thinking or feeling at that particular moment, and through the movement and plasticity of your body.

In exploring the score in detail, however, you must not lose sight of the eventual aim which is to create a coherent interpretation where all the details have their place and balance within the whole. Here your intuition may well be your strongest asset. Use it. Listen to it. Your intuitive feeling for what the music and text are expressing is every bit as important as your intellectual or academic understanding of it. There is no point in being accurate to the smallest semiquaver (sixteenth-note) if as a result you do not sense the tempo or feel the style of the music. In the same way, it makes no sense paying attention to the most minuscule musical signpost if as a result you misunderstand the whole character. For this reason it is often helpful when interpreting a score to sing through sections you have been working on. This not only provides relief after a period of detailed practice but will also remind you that the aim is to create a coherent whole for the audience. At the same time, it is important not to continue singing through pieces past the point where mistakes are becoming ingrained. They will be harder to notice and correct at a later stage.

Most performers find it helpful to mark their score, either using words or a series of invented symbols to bring their attention to the signposts. The process of learning a score is also the process of assimilating what these words and symbols might signify in terms of your life on stage as a character. With this in mind you might consider the following questions applicable to the repertoire:

1 How has the composer created the mood of the piece? How have they have used rhythm, harmony, tonality, orchestration, word setting, dynamics, silences, musical style and idiom?
2 Within this, how has the composer drawn our attention to significant dramatic moments or ideas?

3 How does the music of the orchestra influence the building of your interpretation and define the parameters within which you make interpretative choices? For example:

- Are there moments when your singing is unaccompanied? If so, how free can you be with the tempo and how will this freedom influence your expression of the character in situation?
- What role does the orchestral accompaniment play in suggesting to the spectator a picture larger than your own particular character's concerns? Is the orchestra supporting or acting as a counterpoint to your emotion? How might this influence your thoughts and reactions?

4 How does the music of other characters influence the building of your interpretation and the freedom you have to make interpretative choices? For example:

- Are there other characters on stage singing either the same text or the same melody as you at the same time? If so, particular attention should be paid to accuracy of rhythm, dynamics and pitch.
- What signposts are other performers likely to identify in their work on interpretation and how might these affect your own interpretation?

5 What are the dramatic implications of where and how you take a breath?

6 What signposts are helpful indications as to dramatic intent? Are there clues as to the subtext of the lines being sung or the dramatic purpose that your character is expressing in their singing?

7 Are any ideas emerging as to how you might relate particular signposts to your character's gesture and body movement (see Chapter 5)?

For specific ideas relating to the interpretation of text read the section below entitled *The Relationship between Text and Music*.

In order to form a coherent musical interpretation you cannot avoid confronting the issue of what, if anything, the music is 'saying' or what, if anything, the composer is trying to say at any given moment in the music. Musical aesthetics encompasses the academic study of this field of specialisation which you will encounter more pragmatically through the advice you receive or in the research you undertake as preparation for a role.

Musical thinkers are divided as to whether or not music has the power to communicate as opposed to stimulate. There are very broadly two main bodies of opinion represented by the 'absolutists' and the 'referentialists'. The referentialists believe that music communicates to us through the associations we make between musical symbols and things outside of music. For example, a harp may be used to signify peacefulness, or a particular chord may be used to signify a particular character. In this way music communicates through the vocabulary of references already shared by composer and listener or through references established by the composer in the course of a particular piece, for example, through the use of *leitmotif*. As listeners we are particularly exposed to these ideas through film music and advertising.

The absolutists, on the other hand, believe that music does not mean anything in itself. It stimulates feelings in the listener, provokes an inner sense of revelation or a moment of truth that is beyond signs and symbols. In this way an empathy exists between the music naturally inside us and the music we are listening to. Emotion is stimulated through a shared imaginative experience.

Music in sung theatre has the opportunity to work in both these ways. However, the music will always affect the world of the drama. Everything you sing can be related to something outside the music primarily because everything you sing is related to your character and their situation. In this way music can be thought of as the camera through which the audience observes the unfolding drama. Therefore different musical choices will affect the way in which the audience views the action on stage and consequently affect the different emotions stimulated within the audience. Musical directors and singing coaches are there to give their advice with regard to what the music is saying. However, their advice may not always coincide with your own instinctive ideas. Opinions and ideas in this area tend to be personal and passionately held, reflecting consciously or unconsciously a position taken within the debate outlined above.

Within the context of this debate you must guard against too literal an attitude to the significance of signposts both musically and dramatically, i.e. 'If the music is doing x then the drama *must* do y.' On the other hand, you should beware of assuming that executing the music as it appears in the score will constitute an interpretation. What is written in the score is usually no more than a skeleton, a pale imitation of the composer's original inspiration. Recognising the signposts is only the first stage. When you ask what those signposts mean either to yourself or the composer then the process of interpretation has truly begun.

In assuming that a composer has given significance to a particular moment in the music, it is also possible that you will, consciously or unconsciously, choose to 'ignore' it. This may serve to reveal other moments of significance hitherto unexplored. However, this also places an extra responsibility upon you to create a focused, coherent interpretation. If not the audience may hear two conflicting versions, the composer's and your own. The danger is that these versions may cancel each other out.

As a creative artist you are asking the question: 'What do I want to say?' As an interpretative artist the question is: 'What does the composer want me to say?'

EXERCISE 70

Title: What's Going On?

Destination: Awareness

Via: Listening, concentration, imagination

Risk: Low

Resources: Recorded music and cassette player

1 Musical accompaniment and instrumentation can, among other things, suggest mood, atmosphere, emotion and character. Concentrated listening can train the ear to hear things in an accompaniment that may then be harnessed by the performer for musical and dramatic interpretation.

Instructions[1]

a. Close your eyes. Play a song with an orchestral accompaniment. Pay attention to the words. Are they clear? If they are in a foreign language that you do not understand, can you get a general sense of what they mean from the music and the way in which they are articulated? If the song is from an opera or a musical, can you guess what the dramatic situation might be or why the song is being sung?

b. Play the song again. This time pay attention to the orchestration. What instruments are playing? Why has the composer or orchestrator chosen these instruments? How do the instruments chosen affect the mood of the piece in your mind? Does this affect the way you perceive the character singing? If the instrumentation were different how might that affect your perception of the character? Is the accompaniment loud or soft? Are there many instruments playing at the same time or is the piece sparsely orchestrated? What effect does that have? Are there rhythmic patterns in the accompaniment? Which instruments play them? What effect do these rhythmic patterns have? How do they add to your understanding of what the dramatic situation might be? Did the words suggest a dramatic situation? Was there an accompaniment all the time? Why might the composer choose to have no accompaniment?

c.   Listen to the song again. This time pay attention to the vocal line. Does the melody have similar rhythmic patterns to the accompaniment? Is the range of the melody large or is it confined to just a few notes? Why might a composer want to confine a melody to just a few notes? Are there large leaps between notes? What do you notice about the words at these moments? Is the melody part of one dynamic? Are there many quick contrasts of pitch and intensity or do these dynamics change gradually? How do these observations help you to form a picture of a dramatic situation?

THE RELATIONSHIP BETWEEN TEXT AND MUSIC

One of the most creative tasks for the performer of sung theatre when interpreting a score is to bring the relationship between text and music alive. And yet the very idea of characters singing words in a dramatic situation without seeming (for the most part) to recognise that they are singing is a strange convention to ask the audience to accept, if only because we tend to talk rather than sing when we converse in daily life.

It is often said that those moments when the character's passion grows beyond the bounds of the everyday are more suited to song. At such moments it is as if speaking the words is not enough. Certainly this may be a useful idea to have in mind when moving from spoken text (as in a monologue or dialogue) to sung text (as in a song or duet) or from recitative to aria. However, sung theatre is more than this.

By entering the world of music the text can achieve contrasts in rhythm, pitch and dynamics that are greater than those within spoken theatre. The score is in itself an expression of music's

119

capacity to organise sounds and rhythms so that many musical events take place at the same time. Harmony and counterpoint are naturally created from this organisation. To create an interpretation you must not only be aware of a horizontal coherence (i.e. a coherence over the period of time the performance lasts), but also of a vertical coherence (i.e. your role in the creation of harmony and counterpoint). Text, and consequently the drama, is greatly affected by the vertical coherence that music requires to satisfy its potential with the result that word and music can combine to create a new reality. This is connected to, but independent of, the dictates of everyday reality. It allows us to blur the line between the worlds of the daily and the marvellous. The performer of sung theatre is released by a stylised form to move more freely between different planes of consciousness, between the worlds of reason and feeling, reality and surreality, the private and the public, the subconscious and the conscious. In doing so you are responsible for bringing together your character's desire to express with the art itself of expressing, finding a way of presenting who we are and what we are (truthfulness to life) through the means of a theatrical truth (stylisation). The art of expressing when acting in sung theatre differs from that of spoken theatre. For example, you may find yourself interacting with other characters who are:

- Singing the same text, singing the same rhythm, singing the same melody.
- Singing the same text, singing the same rhythm, singing a different melody.
- Singing the same text, singing a different rhythm, singing a different melody.
- Singing a different text, singing the same rhythm, singing the same melody.
- Singing a different text, singing the same rhythm, singing a different melody.
- Singing a different text, singing a different rhythm, singing a different melody.

In any of the above, each character's actions will most likely be subject to different motivations. At any point therefore the precision required for the music to cohere may be in conflict with the truthfulness required to sustain your own character's drama in an ensemble.

The boundaries between text and music are less distinct than might at first appear. We can think of words, in the way they relate to music, as tools to make ideas, thoughts and feelings more concrete. We can think of music, in the way it relates to text, as providing a more abstract dimension to character, emotion and situation. However, we can also think of words as sounds with a musicality of their own which you can use to communicate in a more visceral way, feeling the inherent quality and substance of the word as an integral part of its meaning.

It is necessary to find the right balance between word and sound, between articulation and expression. Beware of hearing the sound you produce as something that is separate from the word. You risk losing the sense of the word. Through a commitment to language you can unlock the true expressive power of sound. For this reason it is vital that at each moment you use your thoughts and feelings to connect the words and action with the music, allowing the word to affect the sound.

EXERCISE 71

Title: Animals

Destination: Singing and listening

Via: Concentration, trust

Risk: Low/medium

Resources: None

Instructions[2]

a. Find a partner and between you choose an animal, bearing in mind that you must both be able to do a passable vocal imitation of that animal.[3]

b. Now close your eyes and begin to walk slowly around the room moving away from your partner.[4]

c. On a signal from the leader start to make your sound. Find your partner without opening your eyes.

2 A performer needs to develop the co-ordination required to give and receive information at the same time, principally the ability to sing and listen simultaneously. This and a number of the exercises that follow practise this act of co-ordination.

3 The leader will need to make sure that no two pairs have chosen the same animal.

4 At this stage silence is vital. Walk slowly.

EXERCISE 72

Title: Rhythm Hunt

Destination: Aural awareness

Via: Concentration, imagination

Risk: Low

Resources: None

Instructions[5]

a. Find a partner and between you invent a simple clapping rhythm. You must both be able to execute this accurately.[6]

b. Now close your eyes and walk around the room in silence.

c. On a signal given by the leader, clap your rhythm. Find your partner without opening your eyes. When you have found each other, open your eyes but continue clapping until everyone has found their partner.[7]

Variation 1

Each individual has to devise their own rhythm. You must therefore know your partner's rhythm well enough to listen out for it while clapping your own.[8]

Variation 2

Each individual uses two (or more) sentences of text.

EXERCISE 73

Title: Sounding Off

Destination: Group awareness

Via: Listening, imagination

Risk: Medium

Resources: A sung text

Instructions[9]

a. Sit in a circle and close your eyes.

b. As a group you must create a simple 'sound' picture using

5 This game functions along the same lines as the previous one but is made more difficult by the clapping and in Variation 2 by the use of text.

6 At this point the leader will need to make sure that no two pairs have had the same idea.

7 Make sure the game is played right to the end with nobody opening their eyes until they find their partner.

8 Once again, the leader should make sure that no two rhythms are the same.

9 This exercise is primarily about group awareness and is best practised on a regular basis. The larger the group, the more difficult the exercise is to achieve. If necessary begin with smaller groups.

122

either voice or percussion. Any member of the group may make a sound to contribute to this picture at any time, but only one person may produce a sound at any one time. This sound must completely disappear before the next sound can come in.

c. Applying the principle that has been established above, repeat the exercise, this time using a sung text. It should be a text that everyone in the group knows well. Your objective is to reach the end of the text with only one person singing at any one time. Any member of the group may contribute to the progression of text by singing a word, a phrase or a sentence; however, only one person may sing at any one time and the sound of their voice must completely disappear before the next person can come in.[10]

EXERCISE 74

Title: Over Hear

Destination: Aural awareness

Via: Trust

Risk: Low

Resources: None

Instructions[11]

a. Find a partner and stand opposite them. The group should now be in two lines facing one another across the room. Make sure that within each line everyone is evenly spaced.

b. People on one side of the room close their eyes. People on the other side of the room should mix themselves up so they are no longer standing opposite their partner.

c. On a signal given by a leader, the line of people with their eyes open call out the name of their partner. People with their eyes shut must cross the space and try to locate their partner by listening out for their name. They must not open their eyes until they have found their partner.

d. Repeat the game, swapping roles with your partner.

Variation 1

Some people will naturally call louder than others. If this is the case select a leader who must try using his or her hand to increase

10 To begin with several people will sing at the same time at different points in the exercise. However, with practice a group will develop a shared sense and the exercise will flow more smoothly. When working in this way the group should gain a new awareness of the text, partly because of the concentrated energy needed to make the exercise work, and partly because breaking up the text invests it with an unfamiliar energy.

11 A simple listening exercise incorporating the trust necessary to walk across a space with your eyes closed.

or decrease the level of volume. Try reducing the calls to a whisper.

Variation 2

Repeat Variation 1 except that the callers must *sing* the name of their partner.

Variation 3

Callers must set their partner's name to music using the notes *do*, *mi*, *sol* in a key established by the leader. Once again a leader may change the dynamics with his or her hand.[12]

12 What did you notice during the different variations, particularly Variation 3, where the callers have individual objectives and yet are part of the same harmony?

EXERCISE 75

Title: Where's That Tune?

Destination: Singing and listening

Via: Concentration, trust, imagination, co-operation

Risk: Medium

Resources: None

Instructions

a. Find a partner and together compose a short phrase of music to sing to *la* (between five and ten notes in length). You may also use an existing tune.[13]

b. Now walk around the room in silence with your eyes closed.

c. On a signal given by the leader, begin to sing your tune and try to find your partner. When you have done so you may open your eyes.

13 Bear in mind that the process of composition itself, however short, and the co-operation needed to achieve this, are important skills to develop.

Variation 1

Play the game as before with the exception that you have to devise your own simple phrase. You and your partner must know each other's phrase well enough to listen out for it while singing your own.

Variation 2

Get into groups of three. Devise your own tune. You must also learn the tunes of the other members of your group well enough to listen out for them while singing your own. Play the game as before except that now you have to find the other members of your group.

EXPLORING THE SOUND AND WORD ASSOCIATION

The following ideas are some suggestions for preparing to tackle the sound and word association.

1 Speak the text out loud both naturally and then in rhythm. Sense how the movement of the language and the accompaniment set to it awakens the meaning. In particular be aware of the energy that runs through the text. This energy drives you from word to word and note to note. Even each small word is important and may add to the meaning of a more emotive word. Sense the energy that moves you from line to line and from thought to thought. Discover how each line and each thought ignites what follows.

2 Discover and make notes on your character's progress of thought. In other words the thinking and feeling that gives rise to the expression as embedded in the score. Even though decisions here will undoubtedly change during rehearsal, learn your character's thoughts. In this way you will have the freedom to 'discover' them at the moment of speaking or singing. As a result the words will surprise and you will maintain the illusion of spontaneity. The audience will feel that this is the first time they have been expressed in this particular way, released at the moment of singing.

Bear in mind that silences and rests are just as much part of the fabric of text as the words themselves. For this reason be aware of the feelings and thoughts that surround a word. They reveal your character's attitude to a word. Thinking only about the word when singing is rarely sufficient. It encourages you to comment *on* the text rather than express a character's thoughts and feelings *through* the text. Make the words important not self-important.

Finally, there is always a balance to be found between thought and feeling. It is tempting in the emotionally expansive world of sung theatre to intensify the level of emotion at the expense of precision and truthfulness of thought or conversely to analyse the rational as a means of avoiding the emotional. The role of thought is to support emotion and therefore the thought itself has to be sufficiently intense to do its job. More often than not you can find the qualities of emotion *and* reason within the same word.

3 Pay particular attention to the devices of language as a vehicle for expression. For example, be sensitive to the use of rhyme. This you may need to treat playfully (a comic or ironic word play) or gently point (a means of tuning the audience into another resonance of meaning). Also seek out the use of antithesis (i.e. the opposition or contrast of two ideas by using words or phrases of opposite meaning in neighbouring clauses). An awareness of opposites will enable you to point them so that they catch the attention of the hearer. Not only will this help reveal the character's own thought process but also encourage the spectator to find their own position within the drama.

4 Scour the text to highlight the sorts of images your character uses. Is there a pattern to these images? In particular are there any recurring images or thematic categories into which they might fall? An awareness of any pattern behind these will help you to reveal the inner landscape of your character, not only their preoccupations but also the way in which they choose to express them. Allow the images your character uses to really take hold of your imagination.

5 Speak-sing your text. Rather than sing the prescribed pitches, follow the contours of the melody with your voice as if you are speaking but using the range of the singing voice. Explore the range of your voice moving away from and closer to the range of everyday speech. Use the written rhythms.

6 Speak-sing your text. This time abandon the prescribed pulse and rhythm. However, keep a sense of each note being either longer or shorter than the one before. Exaggerate the changes of speed.

Taken together, points 5 and 6 are ways of bridging the gap between the formalised structure of music and everyday speech. You should not feel you are singing notes. Rather you are expressing words and phrases with sufficient intensity to raise or lower the pitch of your voice or to speed up and slow down the delivery of your text.

EXERCISE 76

Title: The Grand Old Duke of York

Destination: Awareness and articulation of text

Via: Concentration, imagination, listening

Risk: Low

Resources: None

Instructions[14]

a. Sing through the nursery rhyme 'The Grand Old Duke of York'.

b. Sing through the song again only this time with one of the following alterations made to the text:

- the word 'down' is omitted wherever it occurs;
- the word 'up' is omitted wherever it occurs;
- the words 'up' and 'down' are swapped round.

c. Now sing the song again only substituting one word for another in each line. This could be a noun for a noun, a verb for a verb and so on. In this way the grammar will remain intact even if the logical sense is distorted. If you are working in a group then take it in turns to sing a line as you move round the circle.

Has substituting words made you more aware of the original choices? Does singing the original text feel more spontaneous? If so, how? When working with more complex material has substituting words made you more aware of the original dynamics and what they might signify in terms of the drama?

Variation 1

Repeat the game at a slower pace and introduce the following:

- Sing the vowels only.[15] Then sing through the entire song, including consonants.

    Has your perception of the weight of the vowels been altered in any way?

14 In this exercise a nursery rhyme is used as an example to establish a method whereby, through altering the original text, new light can be shed on meaning and the quality of language. Once the principle has been established adapt the exercise to repertoire.

15 This may be quite difficult at first and some repetition may be needed to achieve a flow. Try and capture the meaning of the whole word in the vowel sound.

127

Try the same exercise with a repertoire-based text. Has the meaning become more defined?

- Articulate the consonants only. Do the same variation with consonants.

Has this in any way helped reveal how the consonants can be used as part of the thought?

EXERCISE 77

Title: Move It!

Destination: Awareness of the energy behind text

Via: Physical awareness, thoughts and feelings

Risk: Low

Resources: A sung text

16 The object of this exercise is first to release energy through a combination of the body and the text. Second, to underline the need for a physical impulse to bring a character's language and thoughts alive.

Instructions[16]

a. Each member of the group should have a piece of sung text (an aria or a song is ideal) or you could use something which you all know. A chorus would be ideal.

b. Speak your text several times while moving around the room in different ways signalled by the leader. For example, rolling on the floor, jumping, running, climbing and so on.

c. Next find a space and speak your text with different dynamics signalled by the leader. For example, whispering, speaking very fast, speaking very low and so on.

d. Next speak your text as your character, moving around the room. When the character's thought changes you must change direction and move towards a different part of the room. The speed of movement, the volume of your voice and any other dynamic may also change.[17]

17 What did you notice about the number, length and energy of the thoughts? What did you notice about the quality of the words? Were you aware of different layers of thought?

e. Finally, either individually (if everyone has a different text) or as a group (if everyone has the same text), repeat stage c except that you must sing the material.

EXERCISE 78

Title: Word Power

Destination: Awareness of significant word choices

Via: Articulation

Risk: Low

Resources: None

Instructions[18]

a. Sit on the floor in a circle and speak the words of the text through. If you are using a scene involving several characters then only the character speaking at a particular point should speak the text. When you reach a word you believe is important then tap out the rhythm of that word with your hands upon the floor. Other characters may also tap on your character's words if they believe them to be important.[19]

If a word passes before you are able to tap do not worry – you will still have made a mental note of that word, which is the important thing.

b. Now repeat the exercise only this time sing the word instead of tapping. You can sing the words to the original setting (if any) or to an improvised setting.

Variation 1

Choose a theme. Any word connected with this theme is sung or tapped. For example, time, freedom, power, death, love, nature, rhyming words.[20]

EXERCISE 79

Title: Pass the Line

Destination: Phrasing text

Via: Rhythm, energy, concentration

Risk: Low

Resources: Juggling or tennis balls

18 This exercise is based on work by Cicely Berry in her book *The Actor and the Text*. As she points out, the performer cannot afford to take any word for granted. The aim of this exercise is first to make the performer aware that language involves word choices and that certain words carry dominant meanings. Second, to make the performer aware how word choice contributes to the building up of thought patterns. During the course of this exercise notice those words that seem more emotive or imagistic. Also notice those words that bind the sentences together.

This exercise relies on the use of a text familiar to those taking part and is particularly useful for repertoire work. Where this is not possible, use a poem or similar material that the group has looked at before the exercise begins.

19 Inevitably performers tend to concentrate initially on their own text more than the text of others.

20 Talk about the choices made as there may be disagreement and some choices may be ambivalent. It is also worth bearing in mind that in performance **129**

a word may be highlighted or stressed physically (through action, gesture, energy) as well as vocally (dynamics and colour). This gives the performer the freedom to explore more choices than those obviously marked by a musical signpost (i.e. you may highlight a word without altering the dynamic of your voice).

Instructions

a. Find a partner. You will need one ball between you.

b. Find a space in the room and stand at a comfortable distance from each other. You should be able to throw and catch the ball easily and freely. During the exercise you must maintain this distance from one another.

c. Throw the ball to each other and have a conversation. Each exchange must be timed precisely to coincide with the period the ball is in the air. In other words, either partner only speaks when the ball is in the air. It is, however, possible to shorten or elongate words if necessary by any means that you see fit to use.

Variation 1

As above except that you and your partner must use a dialogue (for example, from a duet) which you have learned. You should familiarise yourselves with where the punctuation marks are situated in the text. At first catch the ball on every punctuation mark. The aim of this is to mark each individual thought. Then catch the ball on the punctuation mark at the end of each sentence in order to mark the structure of each thought and gain a greater sense of the dialogue.

If any character's speech within this dialogue is too long to fit into one throw of the ball then the other character returns the ball without speaking and the speech continues. However, in this instance you should still aim towards a punctuation mark (for example, a comma).

If parts of the dialogue overlap (i.e. two characters are speaking at the same time) separate all sentences out for the purposes of this exercise so that only one person is speaking at a time.

BEING PRESENT

In order to engage the audience, the performer as character must be present in every word. Being present requires you to:

1 Pronounce words clearly. Good delivery should never undermine what you are trying to achieve with your sound. On the contrary there is not a single phrase in the sung theatre repertoire that would not gain through a proper and intense delivery of the words.

2 Pronounce words with a feeling for their meaning and find a

proper and intense delivery of words. This will orientate you in the present and align many component parts of the singing and acting process automatically. You must make the audience believe that what you are doing is spontaneous, communicating the concrete meaning of what you are singing and exploiting the visceral quality of the language through the music. The meaning of the words you sing arises in particular from the context (for example, the historical and musical background of the works) and also the subtext. The subtext is the underlying meaning of the text being sung, the unspoken thoughts behind the lines.

3 Understand the word structure and its setting. You must learn to release the character's emotion through the structure of the word setting. For this reason knowledge of the structure is vital so that word and feeling can fit together. You must feel easy with the structure so that it becomes a strength. You must also become aware of and take pleasure in the playfulness of sounds that form part of the structure, for example, rhyme, assonance and alliteration.

4 Embrace the heightened world of imagery. Enter freely and imaginatively into the images, metaphors and similies your character uses.

5 Remember that breath is more than the means by which sound is produced. It is literally the inspiration of thought and feeling. Words live at the moment of singing as a release of the character's inner life, the discovery of ideas and feelings. The pre-established structure of the music makes this all the more difficult to achieve in practice. When a performer uses breath to serve their character's inner life rather than simply to shape a musical line then words and sentences come to life and in turn suggest patterns of breathing and therefore emotions.

Being present is more difficult to achieve in sung theatre than in spoken theatre for the following reasons:

• The pre-established structure of the music. In everyday speech the elements of rhythm, pitch, dynamics and breathing are, by and large, spontaneous products of our expression. The unpredictable way in which we use these elements goes some way to defining our uniqueness as expressive individuals. It is the way in which we use words, in addition to our choice of words, that reveals our personality, what we feel about ourselves and what we (genuinely) feel about life. In music rhythm, pitch and dynamic have in part been decided in advance by another person. This seems to run counter to our natural expressive tendencies. Where we cannot choose our own rhythms, pitches and dynamics for sung words then those same words can sound mechanical. As a result character, emotion and situation lack spontaneity, as if the real drama has happened offstage and the audience is receiving your character's drama second-hand.

In sung theatre the division between music and drama can lead to a formalistic attitude to music that is more related to the concert platform than to sung theatre. The form of music, particularly the need for line and phrasing, can suffocate the freedom that is required in order to give words spontaneity and meaning. An excessive dominance of words can interrupt the musical line and make nonsense of what the composer wrote. In building an interpretation you need to be constantly aware of the dynamic between the words and the music. The central unifying force is the thought or impulse that gives rise to both music and text. The journey of thoughts you make needs to be learned and assimilated as thoroughly as the music and the text. That is not to say that the thoughts themselves become fixed, rather that they become a springboard for your imagination in performance.

- When the work concerned is in a foreign language you are of necessity one step removed from the meaning of the text. You must not only be clear as to what the words mean – with particular attention being paid to unfamiliar words or phrases that require further research – but this awareness must be second nature. And yet working in a foreign language can involve such a rigorous application to detail that in turn nothing is taken for granted.

- Translations throw up other difficulties in that it is more difficult for you to find the original integration of thought as expressed in the music/text setting. The associations generated by the original word/sound pattern have been replaced by a translation upon which you are now dependent. However, translations are opportunities as well. When you sing in your own language to people who speak that language their sense of engagement with text is that much faster and the spectator's reactions that much more immediate.

EXERCISE 80

Title: Heckling

Destination: Awakening the need to communicate

Via: Concentration

Risk: Medium

Resources: A speech

Instructions[21]

a.   Take it in turns to deliver a monologue (for example, the text of an aria). It is helpful to speak this at first and then to repeat the exercise singing the text.

b.   Other members of the group heckle either using words from the text itself or improvised thoughts.

c.   You must try to silence the heckling by incorporating the outside stimulus as much as possible into the energy you are putting into the text.

[21] This exercise is not only excellent for developing powers of concentration but it can also awaken a desire to communicate. This desire makes the words feel special and will therefore characterise the text.

EXERCISE 81

Title: Jewels

Destination: Exploration of text and significant word choices

Risk: Medium

Resources: A piece of repertoire and several coins or pebbles

Instructions[22]

a.   Person 'A' sings a song to person 'B'. 'A's have a number of coins or small pebbles in their hand. Every time 'A' reaches a word that they feel is significant, they must take a coin or pebble from their hand and place it into the hand of their partner ('B').

The pebbles or coins represent jewels, as precious and special as the word with which they will be associated. The jewel must never be dropped into the hand but placed carefully. In order to add significance to a word you may naturally, if appropriate,

[22] Another way to elicit dominant words from a text.

133

distort the rhythm either by placing the word a fraction earlier or later in relation to the pulse, or by using *rubato*. In this case you should still place the jewel associated with the word into the hand of your partner on the word and not with the pulse. Place the jewel into the hand of your partner *exactly* on the chosen word, not a moment before or after. Finally, when you pick up the jewel from your own hand (to place in the hand of your partner), this moment must coincide with the thought or impulse that gives the coming word significance. This thought may happen the moment before, in which case you will pass the jewel swiftly. Or it may happen during the phrase or sentence before, in which case you will pass the jewel slowly. Remember that the jewel cannot be dropped into the hand, however short the time between the thought and the word. It must always be placed with the special care a significant word deserves.

This exercise is not appropriate for all repertoire. Some more violent actions and emotions would perhaps make you want to hurl the jewel rather than place it. However, for all internalised emotions it is a useful exercise.

EXERCISE 82

Title: Somewhere Over the Rainbow

Destination: Clarity of meaning

Via: Diction, being present

Time Needed: 10+ minutes

Risk: Medium/low

Resources: A piano is useful but not essential. A piece of material from the repertoire. For the purpose of this exercise we have used 'Somewhere over the Rainbow'.

Instructions[23]

a. This exercise requires two people, one to perform and one to ask questions. You must both know the melody and lyrics to the refrain of 'Somewhere over the Rainbow'.

b. The performer ('P') starts to sing the song. In between each line the questioner ('Q') asks questions that serve to provoke the next line of text. 'P' sings as if they are answering the questions. Therefore words must be stressed and inflected as a response to the precise nature of the question asked. For example:

23 Repetition at the stage of memorising, repeated delivery of the same words in the course of rehearsal and repetition of words within the text itself can lead to a performers' awareness of what they are singing becoming gradually diluted. The following exercise uses 'Somewhere over the Rainbow' for the purposes of illustration, but any piece of sung theatre may be used. Make sure there is a clear intention behind every phrase you sing. This avoids performer's 'autopilot'.

134

P: Somewhere over the rainbow
Q: Where is that?
P: Way up high
Q: What's there?
P: There's a land that I heard of once in a lullaby
Q: Oh, is that all?
P: Somewhere over the rainbow
Q: Yes, what?
P: Skies are blue
Q: Does anything happen there?
P: And the dreams that you dare to dream really do come true.

'Q' can adopt any tone he or she chooses. For example, whispering the questions. Notice how different tones of voice in the question produce different responses from the performer in the way they treat the text.

'Q' can ask any question they like bearing in mind two things. Firstly, your partner must perform the song in time and so you must ask questions short enough to fit in the gaps between lines. Secondly, the questions you ask should provoke the text of the song in some way. For example:

Q: Where did you go on holiday?
P: Somewhere over the rainbow
Q: Is that up high?
P: Way up high
Q: Why did you go?
P: There's a land that I heard of once in a lullaby.[24]

EXERCISE 83

Title: Tell Me More

Destination: Sustained listening and reacting

Via: Taking the limelight, harmony, holding a solo line, basic improvisation, timing, diction

Risk: High

Resources: Piano or accompanying instrument

Instructions[25]

a. Divide the group into three voices – high/middle/low.

b. Learn Figure 26 with a leader taking the 'solo' line for the moment.

24 If there is a group listening to this exercise they can think about whether or not the performer is answering the questions in the way they sing the lines of the song.

You can also do this exercise on your own. By writing questions that provoke the text as an answer, you can ensure it is alive in your mind. Memorising the questions can help you to be present and maintain the illusion of spontaneity and freshness.

25 This is a call and response exercise inspired by 'Summer Nights' from the musical *Grease*. Something in this song creates a vibrant atmosphere. We have often found that singing a song everybody loves can be as powerful as a whole day's carefully structured exercises.

As well as tackling a number of learning areas and in particular the difficulties of repeated text, this exercise can be funny and self-affirming. Its use of three-part harmony and solo improvisation – although very basic – make this a high-risk game demanding a supportive group dynamic.

135

26 Part of the task is
to make the solo lines
fit into the time
available. As the
confidence of the
group builds so their
words and their solo
melodies become
freer. In this way the
exercise involves
more improvisation.

   Maintain the
precision of the
response at all times.
The discipline of the
chorus is as
important as the
freedom of the
soloists. Beware of
encouraging further
improvisation too
soon.

   As the game
passes from person
to person so the
group response ('Tell
me more' and 'That's
for sure') tends to
flag. Encourage the
group to re-invent
their thoughts before
each line they sing
and if necessary
explore different
individual thoughts
as a reaction to the
text that is being
sung. For example,
encouragement,
disbelief, boredom,
suspicion, etc.

27 This game can be
played individually if
desired. As it is great
fun to watch, it is
equally appropriate
as a group
exercise.

28 This exercise
forces you to
concentrate on every
word you sing, as
you must try to make
sense of the
newspaper article

c. Everyone in the group should think of an ambition they have. For example, to 'be Prime Minister', 'change the world', 'pass my music exam', etc.

d. Each person in the group takes it in turn to be the soloist. Beginning with 'My name's . . .' they substitute their name for the name in the example ('Nicholas'). They also substitute their ambition for the ambition in the example ('write music'), adding this to the words: 'And I wanna . . .' Everybody else sings in reply: 'Tell me more' then 'That's for sure' (see example in Figure 26).[26]

EXERCISE 84

Title: Newspapers

Destination: Exploring the music/text setting

Via: Singing

Risk: Medium

Resources: A piece of singing repertoire and one or more newspapers. A piece is useful but not essential.

Instructions[27]

Using a newspaper article you have found, substitute the text from a piece of repertoire with text drawn from the newspaper article. In doing so you must maintain both the melody and the rhythm of the original piece of music. You should sing to the others in the group and should have little or no preparation time with the newspaper text. You must know the original piece of music thoroughly.[28]

EXERCISE 85

Title: Drink

Destination: Physical awareness

Via: Concentration, observation

Risk: Low

Resources: None

Instructions[29]

a.   Devise a very simple repetitive action. When the leader claps walk around the room, stopping occasionally to perform your action.

b.   When the leader claps again, find a partner, stand opposite them and perform your action repeatedly for about twenty seconds. During this time you must observe in detail the action of your partner whilst still continuing with your own.

c.   When the leader claps again, move off around the room. When you occasionally stop to perform an action, it is the action you have just observed which you must execute.

d.   When the leader claps again, find a new partner, stand opposite them and perform your new action whilst observing your partner (who is also performing his or her new action).

e.   Repeat this process so that three exchanges take place in total.

f.   At the end of the game everyone lines up. One by one perform the last action you have been given (i.e. the action you observed during the final exchange). If it has been correctly observed, this action will belong to someone else in the group. If you recognise the action as your original idea then step forward and perform your original idea. Now compare the two actions.[30]

Variation 1

This variation could take between twenty and thirty minutes. Before the point at which you invent your action, close your eyes and relax. When you open your eyes you should maintain a feeling or sense of relaxed openness and alertness in your body. When inventing your action you must maintain this state, so the action will be built into your state of relaxed alertness. If you feel that the pressure to invent is breaking your relaxed state, you must start again. Play the game again but stop at any moment when you feel your state of relaxed alertness is broken.[31]

Variation 2

This time there is no time limit on how long you and your partner remain opposite each other performing and observing the action. Therefore the leader does not need to clap to signal your moving off. This happens whenever as a pair you feel that you have learned the new action.

even if the music 'works against' this.
   Experiment with unlikely mixes, for example the music of a love song with the text of a football report.
   If more than one person is using the same piece of music it is possible to have several people performing at the same time. After the game has been played, return to your original text and sing it through. Has your perception of this text changed?

29 Giving one piece of information and receiving another is less a technique than a state of being. It requires a relaxed openness that should prevail whatever tensions the pressure of the performance situation may create. The variations break down the game further to build up a deeper awareness of how and when these tensions arise.

30 First time round it is not uncommon for all the actions to be unrecognisable from their original. Discuss what the group felt when trying to learn a new action and perform another. How easy was it to maintain clarity? What tensions arose, both physical and mental?

31 At first the exercise will progress

slowly, perhaps not
at all, depending on
the group. Encourage
focused relaxation.
This will serve as a
reminder to the
group that
performing is
ultimately about
being rather than
doing.

Variation 3

Play the game as in the initial exercise except that, instead of a series of actions, you have to use two (or more) sentences of text.

EXERCISE 86

Title: Thought You Had It

Destination: Exploring nuance and phrasing in the delivery of text

Via: Physical awareness, being present

Risk: Medium

Resources: An aria, song or other well-known piece of material for the variations

32 This exercise is
based on work from
Cicely Berry's *The
Actor and the Text*.
You can use it either
as a group or a solo
activity. Explore the
movement of energy
through the text and
in particular from
thought to thought,
by translating the
movement of thought
on to the physical
plane.

Instructions[32]

a. Speak through your text several times. Move at different speeds and in different directions around the space. Try changing direction at each punctuation mark and then at each major musical signpost.

b. Take it in turns to speak your text with the rest of the group observing. The aim is to stand still when speaking and move whenever there is a new thought or feeling. Avoid speaking the text when moving so that the mind is forced to dwell on the phrase you have just spoken or are about to speak.

c. Now perform the same exercise singing the text as written.

Does the presence of music support or undermine the thought process? What adjustments can be made to exploit the potential of both? How do speed and changes of direction suggest the emotion of the thought? How does moving before speaking or singing encourage you to be more present in what you speak or sing?

DIALOGUE, RECITATIVE AND HEIGHTENED TEXT

The combination of music and words in sung theatre is used in very different ways. Three of the most important are:

1 *Spoken Text.* At times you will have to deliver spoken text on stage, for example in the majority of musicals, in *Singspiel* or *opéra-comique.* At such points you should be particularly aware of where the spoken text is taking you within the structure of the piece. For example, towards a song, a duet, an exit, the entrance of another character or towards a particular emotion. This will influence the way you will deliver that text.

A common concern with spoken text is that the performer may drop his or her energy at such moments. The transition from song to speech can cause emotion to drain from the voice. This is in part due to the fact that the act of singing requires greater athleticism than speaking. When the voice is no longer filled with emotion or there is no musical accompaniment to support your emotion, a void is created for the audience as well as yourself. Find the right energy level in the speaking (although this also applies to the singing) of words, particularly through the vibrations of vowels and consonants and the inflections you choose.

Of course, you may also be faced with a transition from speech to song. For example, a moment of heightened emotion may be approached through the spoken dialogue and, at a certain point, the music will come in under the dialogue until speech finally gives way to song. Here you must work at creating a link through the imagination that supports the intensification of the character's feeling. You will then be free to exploit your use of pitch to reveal the character's inner life as you move from the naturalness of speech to the heightened expression of fixed pitch. In cementing the passage from speech to song, or recitative to aria, you should pay particular attention to the pace of the words. The pace of language in recitative tends to be faster than that in an aria. The note values in an aria are often longer in comparison. If you require a seamless join, it may be necessary to anticipate the speed and weight of the words in the aria or song during the closing moments of the recitative or speech. For example, if the aria is slow you should find a reason to slow down the words at the end of the recitative, becoming emphatic, hesitant or finding any other feeling that will provoke a slower rate of speech. The composer may antici-pate the heightened emotion of an aria by altering the rate of harmonic change at the end of the recitative. If the rate of harmonic change speeds up and yet the aria is much slower, then you must find an appropriate thought or action which would have propelled you forward only to be stopped in your tracks.

2 *Recitative*. At other times you will have to deliver recitative, which is often used in sections of narrative or dialogue to further the plot. In recitative the text is set to music and accompanied. Here you can exploit the greater rhythmic freedom in order to find a style more akin to the pattern of speech. You must nevertheless still be prepared to exploit the move from a more heightened expression (as in the aria) to recitative and vice versa (see above).

3 *Heightened text*. At other times the writing will be far less naturalistic and much more heightened and poetic. Here you are faced with the technical challenge of communicating – both in terms of articulation and feeling for the weight of the words – the meaning of text when the pitch of the music that has been written for it may be much further away from our normal speaking range. You may also find that the text, especially one that is rich with images and metaphors, is much further away from our normal use of language and as such makes greater demands upon the imagination.

You may find that the text repeats again and again without an obvious dramatic purpose. This must be provided by the performer. For example, your character is becoming obsessive and is going mad. This in turn may influence the dynamic shape of the music. In certain arias the problem of repetition may be compounded when there seems to be only one emotional theme. At times you may need to supply virtually all the subtext as the text and/or the music are so sparse. At other times the text and music may be acting as a counterpoint to what is going on inside the character. At times you may simply need to find an intensity that results from the delivery of a constant still emotion (see 'Sustaining a Moment' in Chapter 3). In ensembles where the individual musical lines are different from each other (for example, duet, trio, quartet, etc) repeated text is often used as a means of allowing the audience the time to follow the texts of different characters as this is impossible to take on all at once. However, for the performer each repetition should be treated with a different intensity or nuance so that the audience perceives a dramatic development whether this is seriously indicated in the score or not.

EXERCISE 87

Title: The Translator's Game

Destination: Communicating and interpreting through sound

Via: Improvisation (spontaneity), awareness

Risk: Medium

Resources: An aria, song or other well-known piece of material for the variations

Instructions

a. Two group members, 'A' and 'B', stand in front of their audience. 'A' must speak on a subject in an imaginary 'foreign language' (i.e. total nonsense). 'B' must translate this language to the assembled group of interested parties.

b. During the course of the improvisation you must both attempt to find a coming together of energy and communication such that the observers genuinely feel that they are being spoken to with one voice.

Variation 1

Repeat the exercise only this time 'A' sings the improvised nonsense to the music of an aria known to 'A' but not necessarily known to 'B'. 'B' must translate the sense and energy behind 'A's aria. 'A' must consciously break the aria up into component parts as in the first version of the exercise so that 'B' has manageable chunks to translate.

Variation 2

One person speaks a text while the other mimes it as if to someone who does not understand the language. The mime must attempt to capture the spirit of the speech rather than be too literal. Take this further by introducing music and then music and sung text instead of speech.[33]

33 When working using repertoire, the exercise is best done using more lyrical passages, as recitative contains too much information for our purposes here.

EXERCISE 88

Title: Duet

Destination: Re-awakening an awareness of text

Via: Concentration, listening, improvisation

Risk: Low

Resources: A dialogue or duet

Instructions[34]

a. Find a partner. Rehearse speaking your dialogue or text with accuracy of picking up cues in mind.

b. Now take it in turns to speak your text and before each cue insert a pause during which time you must speak a summary of what the other performer has just said.

Variation 1

As above except that you should sing the material. The summary is still spoken.

EXERCISE 89

Title: Nuances

Destination: Dissociating thought, text and action

Via: Imagination

Risk: Medium

Resources: A sung text

Instructions[35]

a. Take it in turns to speak or sing through a passage of text that is already familiar to you.[36]

b. Speak or sing the text again only this time think and feel exactly the opposite of what you are about to say or do in the text. For example, when character 'A' tells character 'B' they are desperately sorry to be the bearer of such bad news, they must previously feel a deep satisfaction that they have taken it upon themself to impart this information.[37]

34 The aim is to incorporate yourself within a dialogue and in particular to incorporate the actions of others within your own action. It is a useful exercise when repetition has reduced the capacity of the performer to hear, listen, understand and respond to another character. The exercise requires a dialogue or duet that has been learned by each pair.

35 This exercise is designed to increase your awareness of the numerous nuances of meaning achievable through a change in thought.

36 Discuss the meaning and associations of the text within the group.

37 Combine this exercise with the next.

142

EXERCISE 90

Title: Objective

Destination: Consciously incorporating music into a dramatic objective

Via: Imagination

Risk: Low

Resources: A song

Instructions

a. Prepare a song to use in this exercise. Any song will do, although initially pick one that suggests a particular mood, for example, 'Summertime'.

b. A leader will have a number of different objectives relating to another person. Each objective is written on a separate piece of paper. For example, to make the other person feel small, to seduce the other person and so on.

c. Take it in turns to pick a piece of paper at random. Using a volunteer, sing your song to that person using it to pursue the objective written on the piece of paper. The volunteer must in each case try to decipher the objective and having done so must either resist or accommodate your wishes as you sing the song.

EXERCISE 91

Title: Me, the Writer; Me, the Composer

Destination: Awareness of text and score

Via: Improvisation

Time Needed: 45+ minutes

Risk: Medium

Resources: A piece of repertoire and accompanying instrument if necessary

Instructions[38]

a. Ensure that you have thoroughly learned the music and text.

38 This exercise explores the ideas of the composer and the writer. You can also use it as a springboard to study the relationship between music and character (see Chapter 5). The aim is to examine the relationship between the speech rhythms of everyday life and those to be found in music, particularly in recitative or sung speech. You will need to have a thorough knowledge of a piece of appropriate repertoire.

143

39 In this exercise the performer must guard against fixing the rhythms in his/her head before singing. In fact, for the purpose of this exercise, there is no need to maintain a sense of musical pulse. The text and attitude should be made clear through the note values and silences.

After each attempt discuss how the note values have changed in relation to the original rhythms. Is there a moment when the rhythms begin to sound predetermined? Does it require a conscious effort to avoid predetermining the rhythm? What effect does this have upon the delivery of text?

40 This variation is designed to build up an understanding of the melodic choices made by the composer. Any piece of repertoire can be used. Experiment with pieces of different speeds. 'Johanna' from Sondheim's *Sweeney Todd* is a very good slow piece to use. Once again, do not try to compose the melody in your head before starting the improvisation.

41 This exercise uses 'Tell Me More' as its basis, so it is necessary to have played this before trying 'Manifesto'.

b.   You must change the rhythm of your piece whilst keeping the pitches of the notes and the text the same. The new rhythm must be in response to an attitude or given stimulus (see 'Motorway Madness' in Chapter 5 for some ideas).[39]

c.   Return to the correct rhythms and try to plot a journey of attitudes and impulses that would have created the correct rhythm had it been improvised.

Variation 1

Instead of improvising the rhythm, improvise the melody in response to similar stimuli (as above). In this variation the text and rhythms are fixed. At the end of the exercise return to the original melody and plot an emotional path through it that would have arisen from an improvisation in the exercise.[40]

EXERCISE 92

Title: Manifesto

Destination: Spontaneity

Via: Vocal improvisation, musical precision, listening, group awareness

Risk: Medium/high

Resources: A piano or accompanying instrument

Instructions[41]

a.   A candidate for parliament stands on his or her imaginary soapbox to convince an assembled audience to vote for him or her at the forthcoming election. This they do by improvising the text and the melody of their manifesto over the same chord sequence as used in 'Tell Me More'. The melody of the text in 'Tell Me More' can be used as a starting point if necessary. The manifesto speech/song can be as long or as short as necessary but must finish with the words '. . . vote for me!' In this way it is clear to the assembled throng that the speech is over.

As in 'Tell Me More' there are harmonised responses. They happen at the same time as they do in the latter. However, there is a choice of text. For the line 'Tell me more' you can sing in its place 'Please no more'. For the line 'That's for sure' you can sing 'I'm not sure'.

b. Whenever a candidate finishes, the audience shows their support or lack of it with cheers and boos.

Unlike 'Tell Me More' it is *not* necessary for the ensemble to respond every two bars with 'Tell me more', 'Please no more', 'That's for sure' or 'I'm not sure'. However, remember that firstly, should you wish to respond, you must do so at the prescribed moments. Second, the ensemble can make individual choices as to which of the four texts they sing and when they choose to sing it (within the structure already outlined).

When one candidate finishes another one immediately gets on the soapbox and starts again.

c. Next introduce a 'rabble-rouser'. The rabble-rouser is free to improvise heckles from amongst the crowd, which the candidate can choose to ignore or embrace within their speech/song. In singing comments at the candidate the rabble-rouser must be aware that the idea is to add just enough conflict to intensify or initiate drama, while never undermining the musical or dramatic activity. This takes much co-operation and trust on the part of all involved. The rabble-rouser can be chosen beforehand or may naturally emerge from the opinions held by the audience regarding the candidate's manifesto promises.[42]

Though it is not a high-risk game it is difficult, as musical precision and improvisation need to exist within the same context. Build it up over several sessions.

42 In feeding back consider what moments were musically exciting and what moments were dramatically exciting. Were there moments when both were achieved at the same time? Were there moments when the music was strong but the drama lacking or vice versa? Did music and drama ever undermine each other? If so, when and how?

With a more experienced group it is possible to advance the drama still further by setting the action in a specific location or holding an election for a job other than that of MP.

5 Character, emotion and sound

In realising a role in its entirety a performer seeks to behave truthfully in the imaginary circumstances of the story. On this journey you will discover the vocal, physical and emotional language of another person, namely, your character. The exercises in this chapter are designed to facilitate your discovery.

Some of the exercises involve elements of improvisation. Improvising can serve to release you from the pressures of having to combine music and drama and also from the limitations of working only with the text or libretto. In rehearsal, improvisations based on analagous situations offer one way of discovering the significance of a scene from the point of view of your character. However, it is not always easy to carry the freedom of what you have discovered in improvisation over to the stricter confines of your work on specific repertoire. Returning to the formalised structures of music can effectively nullify the good work achieved during improvisation. In sung theatre the ability to build a bridge between improvisation and the more structured work of rehearsal and performance is vital. Making the connection between what you explore and its application in performance requires imagination and questioning.

With this in mind, here is a suggested route for breaking down and then building up a scene or song. Incorporate it into Exercises 96, 97, 98 and 103. Elements of improvisation are introduced gradually. Some of this work will expose the individual. Therefore as a group you will need to support and encourage one another.

- Make sure that you have thoroughly learned the scene or song you use.
- Act out the scene without music (i.e. as if it were spoken drama).

- Act out the scene with the musical accompaniment, speaking the text in rhythm. Try to make dramatic sense of the rhythms.
- Act out and sing the scene, substituting the text with an imaginary improvised language. Try to maintain the emotional heart of your interpretation even though you are using nonsense.
- Act out the scene using movement and gesture but no sound. Repeat this with the musical accompaniment.
- Discuss the scene or song in terms of what your character wants from the situation and what obstacles stand in their way.
- Using the bare bones of the drama improvise, using words and action, a scene where you explore the characters' wants and the obstacles they face to those wants.
- Improvise again using gesture and movement only.
- Improvise again in an imaginary language.
- Use only improvised sounds exploring the full range of the singing voice. No gesture or movement should be used.
- Improvise using nonsense, improvised song and action.
- Return to the original scene and use *Sprechgesang* (speak-singing) and an imaginary language. The *Sprechgesang* should be half way between speaking and singing. It should follow the contours of the original melody though not the precise pitch. The aim is to explore how you can communicate your feelings using changing musical pitch to represent spoken inflection. Keep the rhythm of the original scene.
- Act out the original scene using *Sprechgesang* and the written text.
- Sing and act the scene as written.

  Remember that silence creates tension and suspense. Explore this in your improvisations.

CHARACTER

In sung theatre you are required to behave on stage as if the given circumstances of the material provided by the music and drama were real. It is rare for a performer to have a perfect affinity with the roles that he or she is required to play. Therefore an act of transformation must take place. Behind the more material processes such as costume, make-up and props which may contribute to this transformation lies an act of imagination. In order to

147

provoke and harness the imagination you have to ask questions. Questioning motivates your will and energy. It supplies the framework for your character's behaviour, linking what could otherwise be a series of arbitrary acts.

You may find the following questions helpful when you construct a role. Try keeping a notebook from the beginning of your work on a role to the final performance. Looking back at your notes from time to time will refuel your imagination during the rehearsal process. It is also an excellent way of counteracting the 'second night' syndrome – the feeling that somehow the edge has been lost from your performance.

1 What is the story? What is the story from your character's point of view, i.e. from the perspective of what your character knows and what your character encounters? What has happened to your character before the story begins and what will happen to your character after the story ends?

2 Where does the climax of the story occur? Does this coincide with the crisis point for your character?

3 What would you consider to be the indisputable facts about your character? Upon what evidence are you basing each of your factual claims?

4 What *exactly* does your character say about him- or herself?

5 What *exactly* does your character say about every other character?

6 What *exactly* does every other character say about your character?

7 How would you describe your character in detail? For example, physical characteristics, age, status, and personality.

8 How does the music describe your character (see Chapter 4)? How is your character's music different from the music of other characters? How does the orchestration add definition to your character? Whose side is the music on?

9 What words or phrases immediately spring to mind about your character?

10 What situations in your own life parallel or have paralleled the situations your character faces? How detailed is your recollection of them? How are you different from your character? In making these comparisons beware of judging or sentimentalising your character in any way.

11 What does your character want a) in terms of the whole story

(i.e. the central idea of the character) and b) in each and every scene in which he or she appears? What will your character do to get what he or she wants? Where and how are these wants revealed? Who and what are the obstacles to your character's wants? Are these obstacles to the character's will primarily external or internal? Does your character overcome these? What does he or she do in order to achieve what they want (their action)? Does the answer to this question for each scene differ from answering this question with the whole work in mind?

12 How would you define the journey your character makes in the course of the story? Does the music reflect the different stages of this journey? Identify the musical and textual turning points for your character. Do they coincide?

13 How does your character express him- or herself? Does your character have any particular mannerisms, speech habits or characteristic turns of phrase? How introspective or self aware are they? What makes your character laugh?

14 What would appear in your character's autobiography? What are your character's beliefs?

The answers to such questions not only provide you with the necessary background for your performance but can also help you to define each individual scene. Your aim is to open yourself to the work as a whole. Consider the overall mood of the story as well as the specific moods that characterise each separate section. Most importantly, you must act out (externalise) the ideas arising from your analysis in order to reap any material benefit from it. If not the analysis will remain an intellectual one and of little benefit to your performance or the spectator's understanding of it.

The fusion of performer and role must be constructed on its own terms. In sung theatre you are not as free to effect an identification with character as your counterparts in the world of film or spoken theatre. If you enter too fully into the mystery of transformation, you will abandon the dimensions of time, pitch, timbre and volume as suggested by the score and in performance by the presence of conductor and orchestra. At the same time, when you are constructing a role, music's provision of rhythm and pitch provides a key to your character's inner emotions and therefore can free you from the confines of your own temperament.

MUSIC AND CHARACTER

When looking specifically at the links between music and character it is worth stating that any interpretation of a piece of music is an act of characterisation. In sung theatre the process of finding a character influences musical characterisation. Conversely, characterise the music in a particular way and you inevitably affect your character's behaviour on stage. The relationship between the singing and the acting is, and should always be, reciprocal.

Like the process of building a character in acting, you can approach the characterisation of music externally (from the outside in), or internally (from the inside out). Within sung theatre these two approaches will forge a different relationship between music and drama.

When you approach the music from the outside in, the music acts as a beacon that will guide you towards finding the specific way a character will express him- or herself. You need to accept and trust that what the composer has written in some way indicates your character's behaviour in given circumstances. To offer a simple example: In recognising that the composer has written a 'forte which makes a diminuendo to a piano', you ask yourself how that change of musical dynamics may suggest your character's behaviour or state of being at that time. In this situation you are, in a sense, starting with your feelings towards the music rather than your feelings towards the dramatic situation. This is so even if your musical instincts are born out of what happened to your character in the moments leading up to that dynamic change. Some questions arise from this that can form part of your research, or part of the advice passed on by the stage director and the musical director. Did the composer have specific physical actions or behaviour in mind when writing certain elements of music? If the composer did, then to what extent should the performer, musical director and stage director respect this within the context of the production? Reactions to these issues will vary. In the final analysis you have to feel confident that what you are doing on stage belongs to you (i.e. represents your own interpretation).

Where you work from the inside out, the music is revealed through the character as if the character is creating the music out of their situation and their feelings about this situation. To use the example above as a point of comparison, you explore your character's behaviour at any moment using only the dramatic context as a stimulus and not specifically the instructions given by the composer. The composer's desire for a 'forte which makes a diminuendo to a piano' is then incorporated into the way your character is expressing him- or herself. By guarding the essence of the dramatic and emotional intent, you seek to express an emotion which creates the changing dynamic of the music. In this way musical dynamics become not just an expression of intensity of feeling, but an expression of how much of that feeling is released externally or contained internally.

In reality this division is not and need not be clear-cut. Most performers are flexible enough to use whatever approach best suits them. That the 'external' example is more recognisable as a musician's approach and the 'internal' that of an actor is not as significant as it was once thought to be. It is probably more pronounced in the way that the musical director and stage director work. For example, when the musical director says: 'Can you sing this loudly then get softer towards the end of the phrase?' he or she is adopting an external approach. If those instructions are clearly written in the score by the composer, then this advice is largely a direction to the performer to observe the composer's markings. However, if this information is not contained in the score it is a direction to the performer to create a more musical characterisation. What is particularly useful about this approach is that, in concerning itself with the mechanics of music – louder, softer, faster, slower – it does not impose an emotional intent but leaves you free to find this for yourself. However, if you carry out this instruction without asking yourself how this affects your character's behaviour then you have not taken responsibility for the combined musical and dramatic characterisation. The result will lack spontaneity and personality.

At other moments the musical director or stage director will use the dramatic context to 'unlock' the music. Here the opportunities for musical director and stage director to contradict each other are numerous. However, when these two individuals work in tandem this approach can lead to a wonderful coherence in a production. It may also provide a creative focus for your energy in a way that can liberate you from technical concerns. So many of the issues surrounding the creation of character, interpretation and the advice given to that effect are reliant upon the perception of all those involved, both of themselves as artists and of each other.

EXERCISE 93

Title: Dickens

Destination: Inventing a character

Via: Spontaneity

Time Needed: 20+ minutes

Risk: Medium

Resources: None

Instructions

a. Sit comfortably in a circle.

b. The first person in the circle invents a surname for an imaginary character, for example, Windsbotham or Briskwitt.

c. The second person then invents a first name for that character, for example, Jennifer or Percy.

d. The third person adds a piece of information about that character in the form of a sentence. For example, ' . . . is treasurer of the local ornithology society.'

e. Going around the circle each person adds a further piece of information about the emerging character.

f. If at any point anyone feels that a given piece of information is 'out of character', then he or she can challenge the person who offered it, asking them to justify their idea.

g. Discuss the challenge as a group. If on balance the group agrees with the challenge then that character is 'killed off'. The game then recommences with a new character name from whatever point in the circle you have reached.[1]

Variation 1

Introduce words or phrases that the character might say.

Variation 2

Explore how that character might move. Find the character's voice through improvised vocal sounds. How would they speak? With a high voice or a low voice? In short bursts or long, drawn-out phrases? How do they inflect their voice? How does their voice reveal or hide emotion?

1 At first different group members may challenge anything that does not fit in with their own vision of the emerging character. What must be made clear is that the group is looking at what is possible and not at what is probable. The idiosyncrasies that make up interesting characters tend to be challenged because they do not necessarily conform to conventional ideas.

EXERCISE 94

Title: Photographic Reproduction

Destination: Characterisation through physical observation

Via: Awareness, imagination, observation

Time Needed: 15+ minutes

Risk: Low

Resources: Photographs containing people

Instructions[2]

a. Distribute photographs containing images of people to different groups. The number of people in each group should correspond if possible to the number of people in the photograph.

b. As a group recreate the photograph you have been given precisely, with as much physical detail as possible. Different members of your group may step out at different times to 'direct' the sculpture.

c. Each member of your group has to use their physical position as a starting point to invent a story for their individual character. Use the questions in the section above on character as part of this process.

d. Different members of other groups then visit your sculpture, as if on display in a gallery. They comment on the picture and who they think the characters are. They may also ask questions directly to the characters in the frozen sculpture to ascertain more information. For example, 'What are you thinking?' or 'What are you saying?'

e. After each sculpture has been visited discuss any differences between what you 'intended' and what was 'observed'.

2 This exercise builds on the level of detail required in the exercise 'Dickens' and introduces the performer to character through an investigation of external physical data.

EXERCISE 95

Title: Whose Story Is It?

Destination: Ideas for truthfulness

Via: Improvisation, imagination, story telling

Time Needed: 20+ minutes

Risk: Medium

Resources: None

Instructions

a. Get into groups of three or four.

b. Within each group everyone takes it in turn to tell the others a personal story (i.e. something that actually happened to them).

c. In your group choose one story and ask the person whose story it is to repeat it several times. When listening to the story make a careful mental note of as many details as possible both in terms of content and presentation.

d. The whole group reassembles and listens to each individual member of each group recount their chosen story. Thus in your group of three you will present three versions of the same story.

e. At the end of the last version of the story within each group, those observing must vote on whose story they think it is.[3]

f. Finally, the person whose story it originally was is revealed.[4]

3 This is also an opportunity for discussion regarding the nature of what it is to be or appear to be truthful.

4 Further discussion may take place before moving on to the next group.

EXERCISE 96

Title: Hot Seated Scene

Destination: Building a character, internalisation of character

Via: Imagination, improvisation

Time Needed: Variable

Risk: Medium

Resources: A scene, spoken or sung

Instructions

Play a rehearsed scene in front of a group of observers. At any point the observers may stop the scene by standing and asking you questions about your character, situation or feelings. You must answer the question at once before returning to the action. You must address the questioner directly and remain in character all the while.[5]

5 The process of questioning may initially disorientate the performers. The object is to activate the mind and free the imagination.

EXERCISE 97

Title: Intervention

Destination: Characterisation

Via: Improvisation, imagination

Time Needed: Variable

Risk: Medium

Resources: A scene, spoken or sung

Instructions

Each of the characters in a scene is given one or more 'shadows'. These observers act as a spur to the characters by making suggestions regarding their attitude or action in the scene. For example, 'touch them', 'turn away from them', 'kiss them', 'try to hurt them', 'be intrigued by them', 'bored by them', 'suspicious of them', etc.

Characters must incorporate these suggestions immediately into the action of the scene.[6]

6 This exercise relies as much on the imagination of the observers as on that of the performers.

EXERCISE 98

Title: Before and After

Destination: Continuity of action

Via: Improvisation, imagination

Time Needed: Variable

Risk: Medium

Resources: A scene, spoken or sung

Instructions

This exercise requires a scene on which you have been working.

a. Improvise possible variations of what could happen before and after the scene. In other words before each character enters and what could happen after they exit.

b. Repeat the scene incorporating the new ideas that have arisen as a result of the improvisations.

155

EXERCISE 99

Title: Evolution

Destination: Physical characterisation

Via: Physical awareness, imagination

Time Needed: 60+ minutes

Risk: Low

Resources: None

7 This exercise is a series of practical ideas for exploring characterisation physically. Changing your natural body position and habits is challenging. However, it is possible to re-invent your physical language and combine this with the support needed to produce sound.

8 Working with a new or unfamiliar balance is one way to increase your stage presence. The edge of balance in particular is an exciting, dangerous, creative area. This is possibly one of the reasons why raked stages have become so popular with stage directors and designers in opera.

Instructions[7]

a.   Stand on one leg and reach out with the other to explore the space around you. Now do the same with your eyes shut. Enjoy the precariousness of your balance. Are you aware of placing your energy in any particular part of your body?

b.   Stand comfortably with your eyes closed. Next focus your mind on a particular part of your body. For example, the chest, the forehead, the stomach, the pelvis or the nose. Imagine that an invisible piece of string is attached to this part of your body. Someone is now pulling this string. Explore what happens to your body as you imagine this string being pulled. At this stage keep both feet on the ground until you are 'pulled' so far that you fall off balance. Repeat this several times so that you find the edge of your balance. Then work on different parts of the body.[8]

c.   Now create a centre of energy in your body. This you do in much the same way you have already done. Select a part of your body and begin by putting your attention internally there (i.e. this is primarily a question of mental focus). Allow this attention to have an effect on the way your body moves and then allow yourself to be 'led' by this part of your body, as if you are being drawn from that point by an imaginary force. This time move around the room.

Once again experiment with creating different centres by attaching the imaginary string to different parts of your body. Allow the plasticity of your body to evolve from a sensation or feeling barely recognisable in your body to the most exaggerated and grotesque shape (where your centre is the point of origin for all your actions). Allow your body to evolve back again step by step to its natural centre. It is important that at every stage of the process you feel rather than indicate the physical changes taking place.

Try relating to other performers as you move about the space.

Do you feel a character emerging from the changes in the way your body moves? Do any particular attitudes or feelings arise from this process?

d. Now explore the movement ideas based on Laban's work: Direct, flexible, strong, light, fast, slow (see Exercise 13 in Chapter 2). How do these relate to the idea of a character moving from a centre of energy?

e. Using all the elements above recreate the movement of an animal. Begin by making yourself as animal-like as possible and then gradually evolve physically into a human version of that animal. As you evolve maintain an awareness of the movement qualities you are discovering. These form the link between the most animal and the most human versions of your 'character'.

Is a personality for your character emerging from the feeling of your movement? For example, the gazelle may be swift, agile, even hurried with a high centre. This may in turn suggest someone who is fearful, timid, easily alarmed. A feeling of restlessness may emerge, someone almost afraid of their own shadow, or possibly a predisposition to leap before looking. The hippopotamus may be much slower and heavier with a lower centre. This in turn might suggest someone who seems rather slow on the uptake but in fact leaves no stone unturned. The lower centre may engender a feeling of physical strength, although when deliberately exaggerated this may reveal a clumsiness, a tendency to bungle situations requiring diplomacy and tact. The peacock may have a chest centre suggesting a haughtiness and arrogance, a character who gives himself airs. When deliberately exaggerated this may suggest someone who likes the sound of their own voice, who possibly fishes for compliments but rarely comes to the point or says anything helpful.

ACTING IN SUNG THEATRE

Acting in sung theatre is a creative act which combines the internal and external, the physical, psychological and the emotional in a way that is personal and not stereotypical. A single 'system' or 'method' of acting specifically concerned with this process in sung theatre does not exist. And yet performers are under ever-increasing pressure to improve acting standards. What exactly is meant by 'an improvement in acting standards'?

In the world of sung theatre this indicates a move towards 'naturalism' and 'realism', which we associate primarily with film and television and to some extent spoken theatre. And yet the formalised structure of music and the specific demands it makes on the performer mean that sung theatre can never be 'naturalistic' in the same way as film or television. You therefore need to develop styles of acting appropriate to the specific content and reality of sung theatre. Style relates to the manner of expression and execution of a performance, and reflects an angle from which reality is observed. It is often wrongly perceived as the etiquette and conduct of a particular period or even worse as little more than an expansive style of acting (i.e bad acting). A stylised performance, however, is not simply the opposite of a 'naturalistic' performance. Stylising may involve taking sound, feeling and action that are true to nature and making them more abstract. It may involve relating an abstract idea more concretely to the lifelike while maintaining something of the facility and play of the original abstract conception. However, in exploring any style of performance you must still remain truthful. This does not necessarily confine you to a 'naturalistic' acting style. Truth and sincerity emanate from the performer's inmost feelings. They can only be present when as a performer you undertake to sing and act as a necessary expression of your character's inmost state.

The contribution of the great Russian actor and theorist Konstantín Stanislavski to the development of a workable technique for the process of truthfulness has been immense. Stanislavski's work on finding and reproducing moments of spontaneity has laid the foundation for a modern approach to the actor's craft. His ideas, referred to as the 'System', apply to many of the challenges faced by the performer in sung theatre and not just to the 'naturalistic' or 'realistic' acting style most often correlated with these ideas. For example, his ideas on finding the 'given circumstances' that act as a mainspring for a character's behaviour, on the need for an inner justification for what a performer is doing at any moment, on the 'Object of Action' towards which a performer's inner vision is trained, and on exploring the singularity of the characters that make up a mass. These are as applicable to sung theatre as they are spoken theatre. In fact Stanislavski's work is fascinating precisely because it goes beyond psychological states to embrace the area of physical action so important to expression in sung theatre. Through its focus on the conditions for 'truth' on stage it remains one of the most valuable theoretical explorations of the actor's craft a performer has.

The work of Vsevolod E. Meyerhold, whose 'stylised' theatre Stanislavski encouraged, is also interesting. His theory of 'bio-mechanics' investigated the suppleness of expression in the human body in an attempt to provoke a reflex in the spectator which relied on kinesthetics, or the sense of motion. In doing so he recognised that the union between vocal and physical rhythms could be broken so that the actor did not simply allow the body to follow the rhythm of the words (or music). The object was to move towards a rhythm more specific for the stage. Meyerhold's work only touches on specific theories for sung theatre but in many cases it is possible to interpolate 'singing and acting' for 'acting'. Meyerhold's process of allowing the actor to separate out different levels, work independently on each of them, and reintegrate them in the result, is an idea that has found its way into this book.

Antonin Artaud, Bertolt Brecht and Jerzy Grotowski have all influenced theatre since Stanislavski and Meyerhold. While all of them are primarily concerned with spoken theatre, they have nevertheless left behind useful ideas when exploring styles of acting appropriate to the sung theatre repertoire. Artaud's work reminds us that what the audience sees is also part of what it feels and believes. For example, in the idea that for every thought or feeling that a character has, there is a corresponding breath that relates to its expression. Brecht explores the idea of combining truthfulness in performance with that of stepping aside from the character to provide a sort of commentary. This notion of dis-tancing while sustaining believability reflects issues at the heart of maintaining vocal quality and emotional intensity. Grotowski's work places a premium on the relationship between actor and spectator. His work is particularly interesting for the way it uses exercises to free the actor from blocks that act as a barrier between inner impulse and external expression. Finally there is the work of Eugenio Barba which explores underlying principles of the performer's technique across time and across cultures. In doing so it reveals many possible points of departure (for example, the use of balance, stage presence, energy, use of the hands, feet, face and eyes) in the exercising and development of your craft.

The exercises we have used and developed draw upon these influences. If you want to research further, source material is listed in the bibliography.

EXERCISE 100

Title: Switch Back

Destination: Stylising

Via: Extending and compressing

Time Needed: 15+ minutes

Risk: Low/medium

Resources: None

Instructions

a. Get into pairs ('A' and 'B'). 'A' begins an action. For example, reading a book or writing a letter. This action should be as naturalistic in detail as possible. 'B' observes.

b. On a signal from the leader 'A' and 'B' switch. 'B' must now pick up 'A's mime and begin to exaggerate or extend its qualities. For example, size, speed, texture, weight, etc.

c. The exercise continues with 'A' and 'B' switching back and forth until the mime has grown to ridiculous proportions. For example, the book is now ten metres wide or the pen is now ten feet high.

d. Begin the exercise again. This time try diminishing or compressing the qualities of the mime.

Variation 1

As above only this time your mime centres on expressing an emotion through the face. Begin once again with a naturalistic facial mask and extend or compress through the face as you switch to and from your partner.[9]

9 The most obvious danger here is that you may be tempted to 'mug' the emotion, simply copying the effect as expressed in your partner's face. If this occurs spend more time observing before switching. You should also develop the area of emotional access, as this will facilitate exploration.

EXERCISE 101

Title: Peanut Vendor

Destination: Singing and listening, simultaneously imparting and receiving information

Via: Eye-contact, concentration, co-operation, co-ordination, spatial awareness, role-play, diction, clarity, holding a vocal line, harmony singing, timing

Time Needed: 30+ minutes

Risk: Medium

Resources: Piano and resource cards (see examples below)

Instructions[10]

The exercise requires preparation on the part of the leader. You will need as many postcards as there are members of the group, but the final number must be divisible by three. You will also need a matching set of three cards to use for demonstration purposes. Create the necessary number of sets by writing a number and the text that goes with it on separate postcards. You may use examples from the list below:

A1	I need to cut my hair
B1	I can give you a curly perm
C1	Scissors!
A2	I need to cook a meal
B2	I can give you some olive oil
C2	Saucepan!
A3	I need to mend my bike
B3	I can give you a puncture kit
C3	New wheel!
A4	I need to have a wash
B4	I can give you a bar of soap
C4	Shower!
A5	I need to learn to drive
B5	I can give you a lesson now
C5	L-plate!
A6	I need to make a bed
B6	I can give you a change of sheets
C6	Pillow!
A7	I need a holiday
B7	I can give you a charter flight
C7	Passport!
A8	I need to walk the dog
B8	I can give you a leather lead
C8	Fido!

10 This exercise is a find-your-partner game and incorporates many of the skills hitherto developed. As such it can be played over and over again, concentrating on a different area of performance technique each time. The music comes from the Cuban song 'The Peanut Vendor'.

161

11 You may wish to explain the differences between the three sets of cards, i.e. 'I need . . .', 'I can give you . . .', 'Something' (a two syllable word). However, each group should keep the contents of their cards secret from the other groups. Within each group it does not matter if people see each other's card.

12 At this stage an example is used to avoid the other groups hearing the individual phrases before the exercise begins in earnest.

13 One group will have to do this at a time. The other groups can put their fingers in their ears while this takes place so that they do not hear the other group's text at this stage.

14 Take time over stages c–f. Do not move on until you are satisfied that the tune has been well learned.

15 Within this exercise the leader can choose to focus on a particular learning area. For example, diction and eye-contact tend to be forgotten amidst the general exuberance.

A9	I need to save my soul
B9	I can give you a book of prayers
C9	Sinners!
A10	I need to make a film
B10	I can give you a starring role
C10	James Dean!
A11	I need to build a house
B11	I can give you a ton of bricks
C11	Mortar!
A12	I need to drink some blood
B12	I can give you a lovely neck
C12	Vampire!

a. Divide into three equal groups. Each group has a letter, either 'A', 'B', or 'C'.

b. 'A' cards go to group 'A', 'B' cards to group 'B' and so on.[11]

c. Each group learns their tune separately, using the words in brackets in Figure 28. The words on every individual card will fit the music exactly.[12]

d. When you know your melody, try singing with the words on your card.[13]

e. Once you know your line from memory give your card back in.

f. Finally, before playing starts for real, everyone should sing their tune to 'La'. This will familiarise you with the effect of all three melody lines going at once.[14]

g. After an accompaniment is established on the piano, you will get a count-in of four beats to start singing. Each person must find the other two people that will make up a set of three. For example: 'I need (to cut my hair); I can give you (a curly perm), (Scissors!).' To do this you must circulate in the space singing your line and *at the same time* listen to the other lines.

When you have found your partners you must all keep singing until everyone else has found their two partners.[15]

Group members may also stop singing in order to listen to other members, speak their lines to communicate the information rather than singing or to stick their ear towards people's mouths to hear better. If this happens, the exercise is not achieving its purpose. Let the exercise conclude, make the necessary observations and replay the game. If desired cards can be re-distributed so that each person has the same musical line but different words.

As the exercise develops, explore characterisation. The simple words allow you to create any type of character. Discover the individuality of your character while remaining part of an ensemble.

Taken further, this game permits the exploration of physical and vocal characterisation as a framework for expressing the character's interior life.

Variation 1

This time imagine that you are characters in a market. Individual characterisation and attention to the details of life observed are key elements of this improvisation.[16]

GESTURE

The performer of sung theatre in the twentieth century is seen by the audience literally in a different light. The use of candles and oil lamps, which required a more melodramatic language of gesture in the past, has been replaced by electricity and the sophisticated technology of the lighting rig. This has in turn increased the range of gestural possibilities open to you.

Gesture remains an important part of your expression of character and emotion. It must adapt to the demands of the smallest and largest of venues and to the style of repertoire you are performing. You will call upon gesture particularly when indicating something (here/there), when reacting to something (positive/negative) or when describing something. These of course often combine.

Gesture and sound can easily occupy, as it were, the same frequency (see Chapter 3). When this happens not only is the potential for drama diminished but also the result can seem mechanised.

The following exercises explore gesture and you should use them in conjunction with the ideas presented in Chapter 3. Be aware that balance, eye focus, energy and general plasticity of the body are vital parts of any work you do on gesture.

16 This variation also raises issues concerning clarity of intent on stage. A high degree of spatial awareness can be developed, especially in the ability of the performers via an outside eye – stage director – to focus the attention of the audience on a particular character while maintaining the dynamic of the group.

EXERCISE 102

Title: Commedia

Destination: Exploring a language of gesture

Via: Emotion, thought process, dissociation

Time Needed: 30+ minutes

Risk: Low

Resources: None

Instructions[17]

17 This exercise is based on an idea from *commedia dell'arte*. It explores the idea that the emotion behind an action can be made clearer by gesturing to where in the body the feeling emanates from and returns to. For example, with the phrase 'I love her' the gesture may begin from and return to the area of the heart. This idea can be developed through dissociation (using a gesture that seems at odds with the text) to reveal a subtext or your character's hidden agenda. For example, the gesture for 'I love her' may begin from the pelvis (suggesting sexual desire).

a. In this exercise some of the group observe while others perform. Those performing explore gestures of 'giving' and 'taking' with their hands. At this stage it is not necessary to have any particular premeditated thought to motivate your gesture. Think instead of simply starting your gesture from ('giving') and returning to ('taking') different parts of your body. For example, the head, heart, stomach and pelvis.

Those observing make notes on where your gestures started, where they finished, their speed and weight. Using these notes as a guide, observers then comment on what they thought specific gestures indicated. For example: Head (thoughts), heart (love), stomach (visceral emotions), pelvis (lust)?

b. Prepare a series of simple lines that reveal something a character might think in relation to another character. For example, 'I love you', 'I need you', 'I hate you', 'I am furious with you', 'If only I hadn't . . .', 'I can't get my head round this right now', 'What are my options?' etc. You may also use text from arias or songs. Write these lines on pieces of paper and put them in a hat.

c. Take it in turns to pick out a piece of paper from the hat and then say that line as if you really mean it. At the same time find a giving gesture that begins from one part of the body and a taking gesture that returns your hand to that or another part of the body. Your gesture should support the text. For example, 'I love you' – your hand begins from and returns to the area of the heart.

d. Prepare a series of simple lines that could reveal a hidden agenda or subtext for the lines you have spoken. For example: 'I want to make love to that person by the end of today', 'I want to teach that person a lesson', 'I want my money back', 'I want that person to see how powerful I am', etc. Write these lines on a piece of paper and put them in a hat.

e. Take it in turns to pick out a piece of paper from the hat. Now say your original line in the same way as before only this time try and suggest the subtext written on the second piece of paper through your gesture. Pay particular attention to where the gesture comes from and where it returns to. For example, 'I love you' (text) / 'I want to make love to you' (subtext) – your hand begins and returns to the area of your pelvis.

Variation 1

As above though focusing on the dynamic quality behind a gesture. For example, dabbing, wrenching, flicking, caressing, pressing, floating, chopping, squeezing.

EXERCISE 103

Title: Bitter Sweet

Destination: Exploring a relationship between music and gesture

Via: Dissociation

Time Needed: 20+ minutes

Risk: Low

Resources: Recorded music, a list of lines drawn from songs or arias

Instructions[18]

a. Listen to different recorded excerpts of music during which you improvise mimed scenes based on daily activities. For example, cooking dinner or buying a ticket to the opera. You should allow your gestures to match the flow and pulse of the music. For example, loud music – strong gesture, slow music – slow gesture.

b. Now repeat the exercise only this time you have to dissociate the language of your gesture from the dynamics of the music. For example, fast music – slow, pensive gesture.

c. Next write down a series of lines taken randomly from repertoire material. A leader reads out a line and you must say that line with a gesture that seems appropriate. For example, 'It fills me with happiness beyond compare' – hands clasped to the heart.

18 A character's gesture and his/her utterance can operate on different frequencies. This can add depth to the meaning, as a tension is established between what the character says and does. The leader will need a list of lines from songs or arias as well as some recorded music with excerpts containing examples of 'atmospheric' music.

165

d.   Now repeat except that this time the gesture is dissociated. For example, 'It fills me with happiness beyond compare' – fingers scratching the scalp.

e.   Now repeat stages c–d only this time singing the lines.

EXERCISE 104

Title: Timing

Destination: Timing a gesture

Via: Rhythm

Time Needed: 15+ minutes

Risk: Low

Resources: An aria, song or other repertoire based material

19 The aim of this exercise is to explore the effect of producing a gesture at different times from a set of musical signposts, such as the high point of a musical phrase.

Instructions[19]

a.   Work with a piece of material that is familiar to you. Rehearse the action of the song or scene. Those observing should make extremely detailed notes on every gesture that you use.

b.   Using these notes as a basis, work through the scene and every time you made a gesture you should now try gesturing before that moment. Repeat this only now you should gesture after the original moment.

What effect does having placed the gesture earlier or later have? To what extent does timing affect the quality of the gesture or its effect upon the audience?

EXERCISE 105

Title: Wizards, Witches and Goblins

Destination: Maintaining clarity under pressure

Via: Sound, gesture, mime, co-operation

Time Needed: 15+ minutes

Risk: Low

Resources: None

Instructions

a. Face one another in two lines of approximately equal numbers on two sides of the room.

b. For this game you will need to know the following sculptured mimes each of which comes with a sound.

- Wizards stand with both feet firmly on the ground and arms forward (one further than the other), fingers pointing at the opposing side. The sound for wizards is a low pitched growl 'hoh-hoh-hoh' during which the arms move forward and backwards.
- Witches stand on tip-toes with arms raised high, hands pointing forwards and fingers splayed. The sound for witches is a high pitched screech 'ee-ya-ha-ha-ha'.
- Goblins stand with knees bent inwards and hands to the side of the ears opened out so that the palm of each hand is facing the opposing side. The sound for goblins is a low note voiced as the tongue moves forward and backwards rapidly over the top lip (an aggressive bubbling sound).

c. Each side meets up and decides upon one of these characters then re-forms in a line.

d. After a count of four each line takes four strides forwards towards the other line so that each side is now facing the other only a stride apart. It may be necessary to alter the number of paces taken depending on the size of the space.

e. On the next beat after arriving in this position you must perform the mime and sound of the character you have chosen. Immediately one line will chase the other given the following:

Wizards beat witches
Witches beat goblins
Goblins beat wizards.

If both sides choose the same character then you turn on your heels and walk back to your own side muttering under your breath.

If the two sides choose different characters then whichever group 'beats' the other group chases that group attempting to catch as many people as possible before they reach the safety zone of the wall on their home side.

If it helps you can think of this game as a group version of 'Paper, Scissors, Stone'. The object of the game is to maintain clarity of sound and gesture at the point of most pressure (i.e. when the two lines are directly opposite one another).

EXERCISE 106

Title: New York, New York

Destination: Clarity of action

Via: Imagination, mime

Time Needed: 20+ minutes

Risk: Low

Resources: None

Instructions

a. Face one another in two lines ('A' and 'B') of roughly equal numbers on opposite sides of the room.

b. Learn the following chant:

> A   Where are you from?
> B   New York!
> A   What's your trade?
> B   Lemonade!
> A   Give us some!
> B   Here we come!

c. Next meet up in your group and decide upon one trade, job, profession (i.e. something that someone does to make a living). Re-form in a line.[20]

d. Begin the chant and the side that ends with 'Here we come!' moves towards the other group while miming their chosen job.

Although you are free to effect your own mimed interpretation of the job chosen by your group, you must nevertheless be miming the same job as the rest of the people in your group. Furthermore, the mime must be in real time (i.e. you are not allowed to rush to the other side).

e. The other side must guess what the job is and shout it out. When the right answer is given the leader will shout 'Yes!' and the team guessing chases the team miming back to their side of the room. Anyone caught moves to the other side and will need to be informed of the job that team has chosen.

20 The leader will need to know what choices have been made.

168

The chasing/running can only start when the leader says 'yes' and up until this point you have to continue your mime even if you know that the other side has correctly guessed your mimed job.

f.   Repeat as above but with the other side starting the chant.

g.   The exercise proceeds as above.[21]

EYE LANGUAGE AND FOCUS

Eye focus is one of the most important tools you have to communicate with the audience. Without focus there is no purpose as it guides the viewer to understanding and feeling, revealing the thought behind the text you deliver. Directing the eyes is not simply looking with the eyes but is an action that must and does engage the entire body.

Ineffective focus is imprecise and obvious to the audience. The eyes may seem to cloud over, wander aimlessly or even close. As a result the performance may seem habitual, even robotic. If the eyes see in order to observe then you are in effect creating a web of energy between yourself, the audience and the stimuli (for example, a mental image) with which you are in dialogue. This energy will bring your presence onstage alive.

There are many different types of focus available to you and each will combine with text and music to suggest something different. The fixed point creates a tension, an expectation, that threatens to blow up but which is nevertheless retained. It is not enough to stare blankly at a given point – the mind must be working and must project the sense of your thought process. Different kinds of focus reveal different kinds of internal experience. For example, a middle distance focus will reveal something introverted and is a useful alternative to closing the eyes. A fixed focus high into the auditorium is particularly useful for moments of 'vision'. A panoramic focus will reveal a great geographical or emotional landscape. In this way you can use different focus points to clarify the progression of an aria or song.

There are three important points to remember here. First, effective focus works closely with the thought. Most often you will want to call up the underlying thought of a section of text before delivering the text. Sometimes the thought precedes the text by a few bars; sometimes it precedes it by a split second. At times the thought may seem to provoke the music and at other

21 A rule can be introduced that if the side miming reaches the other side then they are safe and can return without being chased. However, the mime has to take place in real time.
   Once again the object of this game is to maintain clarity at the point of most pressure (i.e. when the two lines are close to one another). What tends to happen is that the mime becomes less clear as a line advances.

169

times the music may seem to provoke the thought. Either way focus is ineffective when you are not thinking and imagining. You must really work to arouse within the audience a desire to see the pictures you create. Second, effective focus works closely with the breath. You may need to sustain your breath and focus beyond the conclusion of the accompaniment. You may need to establish focus before the accompaniment has begun. Third, it is possible for your focus to tire. If one fixed focus is required it may be necessary to find a suitable moment in the score to break it before returning to the original focus point. You can also renew the attention of the audience by finding a new image from within which may or may not require a new focus.

Finding the right focus is especially important for passages of coloratura and arias which express one emotion and where there is nothing to help you in the orchestra or where the music is perhaps not obviously linked to the drama. For example, in certain operas it is not uncommon for the composer to have borrowed music from an earlier opera for use in a different situation. At such points you can colour the music with the emotion and find a position on stage, a stillness and a focus which allow the music to create the scene but where the drama does not stop.

EXERCISE 107

Title: Focus Points

Destination: Focusing with the eyes

Via: Imagination

Time Needed: 20+ minutes

Risk: Low

Resources: None

22 This exercise explores different focus points.

Instructions[22]

a. One half of the group explores this exercise while the other half observes.

b. Explore the following focus points without any particular imaginative idea in mind and then listen to the feedback from the group of observers as to the effect they sensed:

- Shift your focus suddenly from one point to another.
- Shift your focus from one point and search for a new focus.
- Shut your eyes, open them to a low/middle distance/high focus point.
- Choose a focus point and reject it, moving swiftly/slowly to another.
- Pick a focus point and allow this to grow in all directions.
- Pick several focus points and look at them getting faster/slower.
- Pick a focus point beyond the walls of the room. In order to do this, mentally remove the wall at the end of the room. Look far beyond it at an imaginary point on which you can fix your attention.

c. Now work the exercise the other way round. In other words, the rest of the group suggests an imaginative idea (a line from a song perhaps) and you must find the focus to suggest this. For example, an object on the fourth wall, something on the horizon, a supernatural vision, etc.

EXERCISE 108

Title: Now You See It

Destination: Exploring eye-focus

Via: Imagination

Time Needed: 15+ minutes

Risk: Low

Resources: A collection of different sized objects

Instructions

Spend some time looking at an object while the rest of the group observe. This object is then taken away and you must now recreate it for the spectator using only your eyes.

EMOTION

In your quest for a truthful performance, you must enter into the world of your character's emotions. These emotions must then find the most efficient and creative way of revealing themselves to fellow performers and ultimately to the spectator. The starting point for this process is the access you have to your own emotions, things that you remember feeling at a certain point in time and in circumstances which were most likely unique to you. Where circumstances are similar to those of your character then you can use your own feelings in order to establish an affinity with the emotions of that character.

Due to the scale of passion explored in the sung theatre repertoire (where often characters not only proclaim their feelings but experience them at enormous cost to the self) you need access to a wide range of emotional states and the courage to express them. Because the force of this expression will be projected physically, mentally and vocally you must be able to connect vocal and physical expression with inner feeling. This is important as there can be a real danger of singing with physical and vocal tension to simulate emotion. This in turn will debilitate the voice. Alternatively, you may retreat away from connecting expression with feeling, in which case your performance will be generalised.

The extent to which you will allow your emotion to alter the feeling and sound of your singing is one of the most exciting challenges in rehearsal and performance. It raises the vexed issue of what it is to communicate more effectively. You will constantly need to balance technical control with your desire to take emotional risks in performance. Only you know your voice well enough to judge when your emotions are liable to overwhelm your technical control in singing. If this does happen then your ability to sing with focus and clarity disintegrates, affecting all areas of vocal performance: breathing, pitch, rhythm, ensemble precision, the overall form and architecture of your interpretation, the quality of voice production, and, to turn full circle, the ability to access those emotions necessary to tell the story. Some isolation of emotion and technique of voice production is necessary.

Once you begin building an interpretation it is helpful to increase slowly the intensity of emotion and to monitor its effect not just on the quality of voice production, but also on the clarity of text and any action which you are exploring in rehearsal. Emotional decisions, in revealing a character's inner life, must enhance the diction and gesture to bring greater intensity, spontaneity and clarity to the overall performance. In seeking a path to balance truthfulness and accuracy, think of the singing voice as a key to unlock your emotions rather than a key to locking them out. The combination of vowel and pitched sounds is far more extreme than the everyday and recalls something visceral and elemental, a link with the most basic expression of emotional need and fulfilment contained in the first sounds we utter. The trained singing voice in its beauty and sophistication should not separate us from this past but unite us with it.

The performer has a further technique in the harnessing of emotion. Where emotions threaten to be too present in such a way that they interfere with expression, then you may distance yourself from the emotion without losing touch with it. In life itself there is often a duality in the way we function between feeling and understanding. We can, for instance, be sad and mournful at a funeral but also at another level be able to take in who is there and other details of the day. You can arouse emotions indirectly by focusing on a specific sensory stimulus. For example, instead of thinking about the funeral itself, you would focus on the smell of incense or a particular vase of flowers.

A vital stimulus to emotion is the music itself. As well as the vocal melodies, you should explore the musical accompaniment to discover the way in which the composer uses harmony, rhythm and instrumentation to suggest emotion (see Chapter 4 for a list of helpful questions).

Finally, what emotion do you want to provoke in the audience? Guard against allowing the music to move you in the same way that you would like the audience to be moved. Failure to do this will not only give the impression of poor acting but of someone who wallows in the sound of their own voice. It is easy to pin the blame on the self-indulgent singer when this happens, but actually it is a further testimony to the irresistible influence of music upon our emotional state. In the end, your discipline must prevail and the truthfulness of your characterisation must be maintained.

It is sometimes stated that music can express only generalised emotions. This seems to relegate music to a subordinate role in the music/drama relationship, relying on the text and story to make these emotions more concrete. It would be fairer to say that music combines with the voice to stimulate common emotions, timeless and universal, at a subconscious level. When filtered through our own life experience, these common emotions become specific. Pragmatically as a performer, there are moments when you need to have faith in the power of music to 'communicate', to give it space to breathe uncluttered by gesture and action.

173

Many writers have tried to decode music into an emotional language, ascribing, as it were, a particular emotion to a particular sequence of notes, harmonies, rhythms or instrumentation. The recognition of a major chord from a minor chord, to use a very basic example, is often explained in terms of a major chord sounding 'happy' and a minor chord sounding 'sad'. Such analysis rarely takes enough account of the unique quality of a performance as something separate from the written work. Nor can it take account of the specific dramatic context within which a particular harmony or melody appears. Some of the most exciting sung theatre arises from the creation of a more profound emotion in which music, text and action are 'dissociated'.

EXERCISE 109

Title: Come Here You Naughty, Naughty Boy!

Destination: Communicating an emotion

Via: Eye-contact, co-operation, role-playing, clarity of intent and emotion

Time Needed: 15 minutes

Risk: Medium

Resources: Piano or accompanying instrument is useful

23 In life we spend a lot a time hiding what we feel, and we learn not to betray our emotions through our voice. Performers re-learn how to betray their emotions through the voice. The following exercises use the creative voice linked to emotional expression.

24 The simple melody and words are intended to make it easier to concentrate on the specific areas of learning.

174

Instructions[23]

a. Learn the words and melody to Figure 27. Make sure the rhythm is precisely learned, in particular the dotted rhythms in bar 2.[24]

b. Find a partner. During the course of the exercise you will sing the melody with a prescribed emotional attitude (in this example, angrily) to three different partners. With each change in partner the expression of your anger becomes stronger.

First time round, you are irritated: imagine perhaps that someone has come into your bedroom without knocking. No big deal but it would be nice!

Second time round you are angry: imagine that someone has come into your bedroom without knocking and you've been caught dancing or playing air guitar to your favourite piece of music.

Third time round you are furious: imagine you go into your room and find someone reading your personal diary!

You and your partner will sing simultaneously. Eye-contact with your partner *must* be maintained and the increasing emotion must be physically and vocally expressed.

c.   When the leader gives a count of four then everyone changes partner. The melody is then repeated.[25]

Variation 1

As the anger increases, the volume must stay the same.[26]

Variation 2

The same as Variation 1 except that this time as the emotion increases the volume decreases.[27]

EXERCISE 110

Title: Keeping Your Distance

Destination: Exploring space and emotion

Via: Awareness, movement

Time Needed: 15+ minutes

Risk: Medium

Resources: None

Instructions[28]

a.   Find a partner and stand at opposite ends of the room. Recall a feeling and then when you are ready walk towards each other. When either of you sense that this feeling is impinging on the other then move to the right and stop the exercise.

b.   Now walk away from each other. When either of you feel that the feeling of the other is no longer impinging on you then move to the right and stop the exercise.

As you repeat the exercise, try to maintain the intensity of your emotion and awareness across greater distances.[29]

25 If possible modulate the key (up a semi-tone). A count of four is also essential to begin.

Make sure the level of emotion increases step by step. It should start irritated and finish furious. You may find that when changing partners emotional intent is lost. Point out that the increasing emotion must be maintained, especially during the search for a new partner. Needless to say, no physical contact is allowed.

26 Increasing the intensity of emotion will most likely lead to an increase in volume. This is a good way to encourage audible, engaged singing. The emotion created is necessarily a more externalised emotion. To compare this with singing a more internalised emotion, play this variation.

27 This is much more difficult, but it can create emotion of great intensity.

28 It is often necessary on large open stages to be in a close relationship with another character although standing some distance away. The object of this exercise is to look at degrees of involvement at different distances with the aim of improving communication

between two or more people on stage.

29 Take breaks during this exercise in order to discuss the results of your work (i.e. what ways did you find to maintain intensity and awareness?). If necessary introduce people whose job it is to act as a (non-contact) physical barrier between two partners. This may help intensify the need to communicate and therefore the expression of emotion.

30 It may take several sessions for a group to become comfortable with this kind of exercise and it is helpful to feed back at all stages. Some may try to resist making 'silly noises', and everyone will need encouragement. With time and in conjunction with other emotion-based work, introduce more serious topics. For example, 'my greatest fear' or 'my hopes for the future'. In feeding back ask whether there were moments where those performing made a connection between the voice and the emotional truth of what they were 'talking' about. How aware is the listener of these moments?

31 The following exercises form a

EXERCISE 111

Title: Converse

Destination: Exploration of vocal sound

Via: Imagination, improvisation

Time Needed: 30+ minutes

Risk: High

Resources: None

Instructions

a. Find a partner.

b. A leader announces a topic of conversation. For example, 'the funniest thing that ever happened to me' or 'my last birthday'. You must converse with your partner on that subject using sound and gesture only but no words. It is important to remember that it is a conversation and not one person telling and the other listening.[30]

Variation 1

Play the above exercise using only sound.

EXERCISE 112

Title: Motorway Madness

Destination: Awareness

Via: Co-ordination, observation, vocal improvisation

Time Needed: 20+ minutes

Risk: Medium

Resources: None

Instructions[31]

a. Get into pairs and face your partner across a space on different sides of the room.[32] The group as a whole is therefore ordered into two lines of partners facing each other. This space represents a motorway.

b. Pick an attitude or emotion at random from a hat. This is the attitude or emotion you will play.[33]

c. Performers on one side of the motorway send a sound to their partner on the other side. This sound attempts to communicate their attitude or emotion.

d. The partner 'catches' the sound and, without letting the energy behind it dissipate, uses the sound to recall a feeling. The sound, which may be influenced by this feeling, is then passed back to the other side and the exercise continues back and forth until the leader calls an end to the exercise.

e. Repeat, only this time the other side begins.

Variation 1

As above except that you are assigned the same feeling as your partner. This is passed between you through a sound and each time it passes from one person to another it is strengthened. This strengthening should not be limited to the vocal but also to the thought that supports the vocalisation (i.e. internally).

Variation 2

Communicate an emotion physically to your partner on the other side who then produces a sound for it. When your partner has produced a sound that communicates what you were feeling then you may meet in the middle of the motorway to verify that you have understood each other correctly.

Variation 3

Sing a well-known song to your partner on the other side of the motorway. For example, 'Happy Birthday' or something from a piece of repertoire you are working on. This song must be coloured with a particular emotion or feeling. You and your partner sing at the same time with different emotions. During the course of the song you must have swapped emotions. The rest of the group observes.[34]

Variation 4

Perform a physical action powered by a feeling that lies behind it. For example, stroking a lover sensuously. When the action is underway your partner on the other side sings 'Happy Birthday' with an opposite feeling from that being communicated by your physical action. For example, deep, intense loathing. The rest of the group observes.

series designed to increase the power to receive and communicate feeling. A list of ideas for attitudes and emotions to play with is given at the end of the exercise. It may be wise to begin with attitudes and progress to more complex emotions.

32 You can experiment with different distances between the two lines.

33 Take a quiet moment in which to recall your emotion.

34 In this variation make the quality of your emotion clear and specific.

177

Variation 5

Sing with a particular feeling, which is then picked up by your partner. When this has happened, you stop singing and your partner continues. They now change that feeling to its opposite. When this has happened you now pick up the feeling and sing. Both partners now singing together must find a blend of the two feelings explored. As above, while any two people are exploring this exercise the rest of the group should observe.

Some ideas for attitudes (i.e. mental states) and emotions (i.e. mental feelings or affections):

Attitudes: Inattentive, sincere, critical, calm, quiet, serious, serene, cool, courteous, polite, insolent, severe, suspicious, facetious, eager, hopeful, inert, languid, bored, proud, contemptuous, shy, pensive, distracted, impressed, confiding, over-confident, remembering, hesitating, apologetic, indomitable, pent up, greedy, neurotic, disgusted, shocked, horrified, scatty.

Emotions: Anger, tenderness, envy, lust, self-pity, loathing, bitterness, fury, despair, dejection, remorse, infatuation, hysteria, greed, jealousy, disgust, frustration, misery, distress, panic, doting, ecstatic, dread, nostalgia, embarrassment, vengeful, threatening, threatened, triumphant.

EXERCISE 113

Title: Wringing the Cloth

Destination: Physical representation of emotion

Via: Imagination

Time Needed: 15+ minutes

Risk: Low

Resources: An assortment of props

35 This exercise reminds us that props can act not only as an extension of character but also as a way of communicating emotion.

Instructions[35]

a. Sit in a circle in the middle of which there is an assortment of props.

b. One by one take it in turns to get up and choose a piece of paper from a hat. Written on each piece of paper is an emotion.

c. You must translate this emotion into what you do with your prop, for example, hatred – wringing a cloth. The rest of the group must guess from your action what emotion you are feeling.[36]

36 It is tempting to use facial gestures during this exercise. Therefore it may be helpful to obscure the performer's face in some way, for example, through the use of a neutral full face mask.

EXERCISE 114

Title: The Television Game

Destination: Sharing the emotional impulse

Via: Awareness, imagination

Time Needed: 20+ minutes

Risk: Low

Resources: None

Instructions[37]

a. In the space place a chair to act as a television screen and several chairs a few metres away to act as a sofa. Define the area around (with chairs or masking tape) as the room in which the action takes place. Identify the position of the door into the room.

b. One by one you enter the space and begin to watch a television programme the theme of which has been decided in advance. For example, a horror movie, the news, a romantic comedy, *film noir*, the weather forecast, etc. You must persuade the audience that you are watching the same programme as the other people in the space. Although your emotional reactions to the events unfolding on the imaginary screen may be different you must all nevertheless be perceived as reacting to the same moment. Timing is therefore crucial and this can only be felt between members of your group watching the imaginary programme.

37 This exercise aims to develop an awareness of other emotions being expressed, encouraging you to be receptive to these while managing the complexities of co-ordination when performing. Use no more than five people at a time.

As each new person enters the space they should acknowledge the other viewers who should also acknowledge the new arrival (i.e. give them focus). Be sure to allow enough time between entrances for the rhythm of the group to settle. In this way the dynamic is built up slowly.

The object is not to catch the other members of the group out. For example, suddenly being terrified at the 'murder'. The only way for you to persuade the audience that you are reacting to the same event is to feel the timing and emotional impulse associated with the event together even if this means progressing very slowly. Therefore you must watch the imaginary programme and

179

at the same time maintain an awareness of what the other characters are doing, thinking and feeling.

Variation 1

As above, communicating your feelings towards what you are watching through improvised sound only.

EXERCISE 115

Title: Cinema

Destination: Emotional recall

Via: Imagination

Time Needed: Variable

Risk: High

Resources: None

Instructions[38]

a. Sit or lie comfortably on the floor. Remember what you did this day until the present moment. Alternatively remember a real event in your life with emotional impact.[39] As you remember you must relate as much sensory detail as possible – objects, colours, smells, tastes, tactile sensations, sounds, bodily sensations, etc – to the rest of the group.

Try not to force your feelings. Instead allow the feeling to emerge through your description of sensory images. If it helps, you may move parts of your body linked to the sensations. For example, moving the tongue and lips at the thought of a cool beer.

b. The group makes notes of your description and if necessary acts as questioners, prompting you to remember by asking specific questions regarding sensory details.

At the end, focus on one object or sensory stimulus that you consider central to the experience. The group may help with suggestions.

c. Focusing on this object in your mind, you must picture it in as much detail as possible. Use the image to recall the emotion you felt when imagining.[40]

38 This exercise is best done with one person at a time while the rest of the group observes.

39 This will depend on the experience and confidence of the performer in question.

40 This technique is particularly useful for creating and sustaining the energy behind a fixed focus where thinking about the original experience is likely to distract. The audience is unaware of what is in the performer's mind. The act of imagination itself and the emotions that accompany it are interpreted in the light of what the performer is singing.

Variation 1

Instead of seeing one object, see a moving picture in your mind's eye.[41]

Variation 2

Using either version of the exercise observers may also introduce fictional events or characters as you tell the story. You must incorporate these into the telling as if they were as real as the other events you are recounting.

EXERCISE 116

Title: Emotional Zones

Destination: Exploration of emotions in character

Via: Improvisation, concentration

Time Needed: 20+ minutes

Risk: High

Resources: A piece of repertoire

Instructions[42]

Divide the room into four zones. Mark the boundaries with coloured tape. Define the four zones as emotions. For example, happy, sad, angry and lovesick. Walk around the space as your character interacting with other characters but expressing sounds and gestures stimulated by the particular zone you are in. When you cross into a different zone you must find a way to make dramatic sense of your change of emotion.

Variation 1[43]

Divide the room into 'situation zones'. For example 'trying to use a telephone that doesn't work', 'seeing someone you find attractive', 'singing a song for the first time in public' or 'waiting in a bus queue with other people'. Use a character you have developed but this time the same fundamental emotional state exists for everybody. For example, happiness.

The object of the exercise is to explore, using sound and gesture only, how your character and their fundamental emotional state change as you move around the space, inhabiting the different situational zones.

41 This is particularly useful for moments where the focus must remain tight but the mind is active.

42 The first variation of this exercise involves sound only and can be used in conjunction with work on characterisation.

43 Emotions are never fixed. For example, every character will express happiness in a different way, depending partly on the situation they find themselves in.

181

44 We are often victims of emotional urges beyond our power or control. Deep, intense feelings can evoke a sense of inevitability that propel a character towards his or her destiny.

Variation 2[44]

In this variation, the room is divided into emotional zones as in the initial exercise. Find a partner and use either vocal improvisation or a piece of repertoire (thoroughly memorised) during this exercise. One person in each pair stands around the edge of the space and either sings their piece of music or improvises vocally in character. Their partner must move around the space from zone to zone, thereby determining the emotion their partner expresses. The person singing must seek to truthfully embody the emotion dictated by their partner's position, however fleeting or enduring these feelings are.

EXERCISE 117

Title: Response

Destination: Exploring emotional responses

Via: Awareness, imagination, observation, clarity of response

Time Needed: Variable

Risk: Medium

Resources: A scene

45 This exercise requires a scene that two performers have been working on, for example, a duet.

Instructions[45]

a. Play the scene once through and let observers comment on the relationship between your characters.

b. Then play the scene through again except that you must begin with an attitude or emotion that is not logical for the scene. For example, a love duet is played spitefully.

c. At each turn, having understood what the other is playing, you must respond either by continuing (playing the same emotion back) or complementing (playing an emotion that will serve to change the emotion being played).

As a prelude to working on an entire scene it may be helpful to explore the idea behind this exercise with lines drawn from repertoire. For example, playing the line 'Someone was saying he's done himself in. Unless he's been murdered!' with excitement rather than horror.

EXERCISE 118

Title: Story

Destination: Improvisation through word, sound and gesture

Via: Imagination, concentration

Time Needed: 20+ minutes

Risk: Medium/high

Resources: None

Instructions[46]

a. As a group form a circle. A leader decides on a title for the story or gives the first line. For example, 'It was a dark and stormy night . . .'

b. Each person round the circle takes it in turns to add to the story. However, you must alternate between using words, gesture and sound to improvise the story. In doing so you should make sure that each new action, whether verbal, gestural or based on sound, continues the story and does not simply translate what the previous person has just created.

Variation 1

Repeat the exercise this time in two lines of equal numbers standing at either end of the room. The story is created as above only it is sent from one side of the room to the other.[47]

EXERCISE 119

Title: How Far Will You Go?

Destination: Expression of emotion through sound

Via: Imagination and concentration

Time Needed: 15+ minutes

Risk: High

Resources: None

46 This is a variation of the well-known game where participants take it in turns to invent and continue a story.

47 This requires even more concentration and the additional energy to project the ideas over a greater distance.

183

48 When the improvisation is being performed, other group members should watch. It is helpful if they know the details of the improvisation that were fixed beforehand. After performing, question the participants involved as to how they felt during the improvisation. For example, to character 'A': When did the intensity of your need begin to sway your partner to relent? What feelings did you have during these moments? What feelings were you trying to evoke within your partner? When did you feel most powerful? When did you feel most powerless? To character 'B': At what moment did you feel the greatest pressure to relent? What emotions did you experience in constantly rejecting someone else's needs? If you did not relent was there anything your partner could have done to make you do so? One general question for participants and spectators alike: Did 'A' go as far as he or she could to express his/her need?

Instructions

a. Get into pairs ('A' and 'B').

b. Each pair invents a scenario in which 'A' wants something that 'B' does not want to give. For example, 'A' needs £500 for a plane ticket or needs to talk because they have just been sacked from their job. A bare minimum of details should be fixed beforehand. These should nevertheless include an understanding of the relationship of your characters to each other. For example, family, friend, employer etc.

c. Next, improvise the scenario you have invented. However, 'A' can only communicate using sound and gesture. You must be prepared to try anything vocally to convince your partner that your need is honest and great. Your partner can only use words and gesture to reject your need. You must both aim to play the situation as truthfully as possible.

d. If 'A' expresses their need so strongly as to make a refusal impossible then 'B' may relent.[48]

6 Conclusion

Performers were the inspiration for this book and it is the performer that we would most like to benefit from the resources it offers. Our intention has not been to define sung theatre but rather to open up its potential. In attempting to do this it has become clear that, contained within these pages, there is the material for several books. The more one says the more, it seems, is left unsaid.

Writing this book has been surprising and unpredictable, challenging and confounding. In recognising this we accept that for some of our potential readers the angle of approach we take and the opinions we express will not reflect your own ideas or convictions or indeed meet the expectations that a book covering such a vast subject will create. We have intentionally cast the net wide to include as many performers from as many different forms of sung theatre as possible. So many more questions arise from the specialisation in one or other of those forms. But we do feel that the issues and disciplines practised in this book are in a very important sense common to all practitioners of sung theatre forms.

There is only one area of technique that this book explores overall – the technique of integration itself. For some performers successful integration of music and drama is simply about managing the vocal requirements of the score. There is no criticism implied here, rather an acceptance that technical challenges will arise from the music which can only be resolved in reference to voice production. Performers who are more secure in the area of vocal technique are generally those performers who are ready to accept the challenges of integration and in particular uniting technique with expression. We are indebted to the many performers and singing teachers from all areas of sung theatre who have given us advice and imparted their knowledge and insight on the subject of voice production. In avoiding this area we have not intended to diminish its importance but rather to recognise that we could not do justice to such a specialised and controversial area. We nevertheless hope that you will find the exercises in this book a useful companion to your separate work on voice production and that they will serve as one stimulus to finding a place for vocal technique.

Aside from the performer (and of course the composer and librettist) the most important influence upon the performance of sung theatre is the work of stage director and musical director. This relationship impinges directly and indirectly on your ability to integrate singing and acting in performance. In earlier times (in opera) it was the composer or conductor who worked with the performer on psychology, emotional expression and even gesture, using an intimate knowledge of the orchestral score as a basis. With the advent of the stage director these tasks are shared to varying extents and with this has come the complication of shared responsibility and a separating out of music and drama. The partnership is not always an empathetic one. Stage directors are sometimes accused of staging a drama that has nothing to do with the composer's work and everything to do with themselves. Conductors are accused of slavishly obeying the composer without feeling for the particular ways in which each production retells a story. Directors are sometimes described as 'music-friendly' or 'not music-friendly' and conductors as 'drama-friendly' or 'not drama-friendly'. Ironically, as the training of performers develops to meet the needs of the profession by embracing training in many disciplines, the division between stage director and musical director is the most visible sign of the division between music and drama in production. Every musical decision the conductor makes has an effect on the drama and every dramatic decision the stage director makes has an effect on the music. For this reason the stage director should study the score and come to an intuitive understanding of the significance of the music and the conductor must study the words, think about the psychology of the roles and come to an intellectual understanding of the drama. If this team is able to develop a genuine co-operation based on a respect for each other's working methods and a willingness to contribute constructively to a shared artistic vision then the totality of sung theatre will be well served. If this is so then stage director and musical director may find a way of talking *together* to performers. This will free you to take your rightful place in the traffic of pleasure and ideas true collaboration in sung theatre brings.

In the same way that sung theatre is not simply theatre plus music but a completely new way of perceiving the human condition, so we believe that the performer of sung theatre is not simply an 'actor who sings' or a 'singer who acts' but a completely new way of perceiving the performing being. The work of the performer, however, is never complete and no performance is flawless. You will continue throughout your life to develop knowledge and skills, and to explore the potential this offers you to communicate. On this journey it is as well to be aware that, however much we look for absolutes, there are none. No creation, whether that of composer, librettist, conductor, musical director, stage director or performer is ever a perfect translation of the initial impulse to create. Inspiration is the beginning and end of a creative chain, and is the gift that is handed from composer to performer to us all.

Appendix

Figure 1

Descend chromatically

Oh_____ Oh_____

Figure 2

Ascend chromatically

Mmm_____ Mmm_____

Replace humming with the following sounds: voom, mum, zoom, zing, ding.

Figure 3

Ascend chromatically

Mmm_____ Ah_____

Figure 4

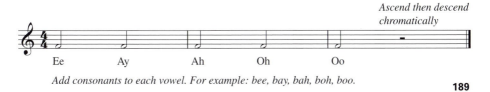

Ascend then descend chromatically

Ee   Ay   Ah   Oh   Oo

Add consonants to each vowel. For example: bee, bay, bah, boh, boo.

Figure 5

Ee   ee   ee   ee   ee   ee   ee   ee   ee   ee_____

Ascend chromatically

Ah   ah   ah   ah   ah   ah   ah   ah   ah   ah_____

Use all the vowels

Figure 6

Ah_____

Ascend chromatically

Ah_____

Figure 7

Dee - yah   dee - yah   dee - yah   Dee - yah   dee - yah   dee - yah

Descend chromatically

Dee - yah   dee - yah   dee - yah   Dee - yah   dee - yah   dee - yah

Figure 8

Ee

Ascend chromatically

Ah

Figure 9

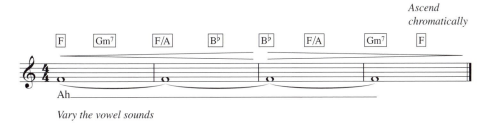

Ascend chromatically

Ah

Vary the vowel sounds

Figure 10

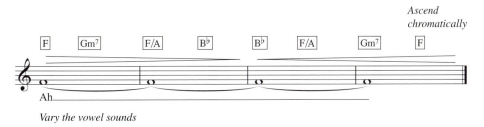

Ascend chromatically

Ah

Vary the vowel sounds

Figure 11

Ascend chromatically

Come here you naugh - ty naugh - ty boy.

Figure 12

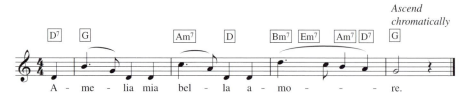

Ascend chromatically

A - me - lia mia bel - la a - mo - - - re.

Figure 13

Peg - gy Bab - cock Peg - gy Bab - cock

Ascend chromatically

Peg - gy Bab - cock Peg - gy Bab - cock Peg - gy

Figure 14

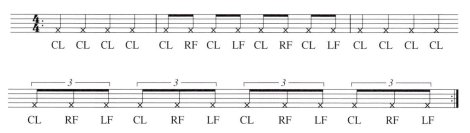

CL CL CL CL   CL RF CL LF CL RF CL LF   CL CL CL CL

CL RF LF CL   RF LF CL   RF LF CL   RF LF

Figure 15

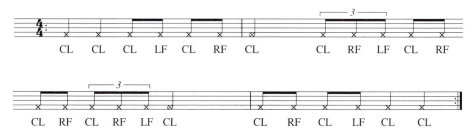

CL CL CL LF CL RF CL   CL RF LF CL RF

CL RF CL RF LF CL   CL RF CL LF CL CL

Figure 16

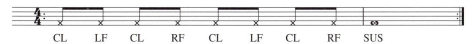

CL LF CL RF CL LF CL RF SUS

Figure 17

CL LF CL RF CL LF CL RF SUS

Figure 18

La la la la la la la la la la la la

La la la la la la la la la la la la

Figure 19

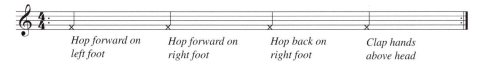

Hop forward on
left foot

Hop forward on
right foot

Hop back on
right foot

Clap hands
above head

Figure 20

Figure 21

Figure 22

The tip of the tongue, the toes, the teeth. The

Ascend and descend diatonically

tip of the tongue, the toes, the teeth. The...

Figure 23

Ascend chromatically

Red lor - ry, yel - low lor - ry. Red lor - ry, yel - low lor - ry.

Figure 24

Figure 25

Figure 26

Figure 27

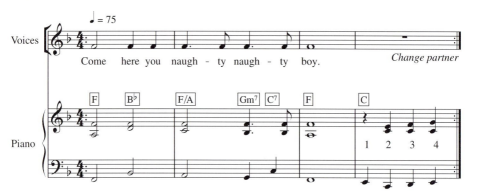

Figure 28

Bibliography

The following is a selection of books that you may find useful. We feel it is important to underline, however, that we do not necessarily agree with either the content of these publications or the way in which the ideas they contain are communicated.

Anderson, B. (1981) *Stretching*, London: Pelham Books.

Artaud, A. (1993) *The Theatre and its Double*, London: Calder Publications.

Bachmann, M-L. (1991) *Dalcroze Today: An Education through and into Music*, Oxford: Oxford University Press.

Balk, H. W. (1977) *The Complete Singer-Actor: Training for Music Theater*, Minneapolis: University of Minnesota Press.

—— (1985) *Performing Power: A New Approach for the Singer-Actor*, Minneapolis: University of Minnesota Press.

Barba, E. and Savarese, N. (1991) *A Dictionary of Theatre Anthropology: The Secret Art of the Performer*, London: Routledge.

Barker, C. (1977) *Theatre Games: A New Approach to Drama Training*, London: Methuen.

Bawtree, M. (1990) *The New Singing Theatre: A Charter for the Music Theatre Movement*, Bristol: The Bristol Press.

Berry, C. (1993) *The Actor and the Text*, London: Virgin Books.

Boal, A. (1992) *Games for Actors and Non-actors*, London: Routledge.

Brecht, B. (ed. and trans. J. Willett) (1964) *Brecht on Theatre*, London: Methuen.

Bunch, M. (1997) *Dynamics of the Singing Voice*, Vienna: Springer-Verlag.

Cole, H. (1974) *Sounds and Signs: Aspects of Musical Notation*, London: Oxford University Press.

Cooke, D. (1989) *The Language of Music*, Oxford: Oxford University Press.

Dunsby, J. (1996) *Performing Music: Shared Concerns*, Oxford: Oxford University Press.

Fuchs, P. P. (ed.) (1991) *The Music Theatre of Walter Felsenstein*, London: Quartet Books.

Gawain, S. (1982) *Creative Visualization*, New York: Bantam Books.

Green, B. and Gallwey, W.T. (1987) *The Inner Game of Music*, London: Pan Books.

Grotowski, J. (1975) *Towards a Poor Theatre*, London: Methuen.

Hahn, R. (1990) *On Singers and Singing: Lectures and an Essay*, London: Christopher Helm (Publishers) Ltd.

Helfgot, D. with Beeman, W.O. (1993) *The Third Line: The Opera Performer as Interpreter*, New York: Schirmer Books.

Hoppin, R.H. (1978) *Medieval Music*, London: W.W. Norton & Company.

Jacques-Dalcroze, E. (1980) *Rhythm Music and Education*, London: The Dalcroze Society (Incorporated).

Johnson, D. (1995) *Bone, Breath, and Gesture: Practices of Embodiment*, Berkeley: North Atlantic Books.

Johnstone, K. (1981) *Impro: Improvisation and the Theatre*, London: Methuen.

Kagen, S. (1960) *On Studying Singing*, New York: Dover Publications, Inc.

Le Touzel, A. (1992) *The Angels Cry*, Ithaca: Cornell University Press.

Linklater, K. (1976) *Freeing the natural voice*, New York: Drama Book Publishers.

McKinney, J. (1994) *The Diagnosis and Correction of Vocal Faults: a manual for teachers of singing and for choir directors*, Nashville: Genevox Music Group.

Matthay, T. (1912) *The First Principles of Pianoforte Playing*, London: Longmans, Green, & Co.

Meyer, (1994) *Emotion and Meaning in Music*, Chicago: University of Chicago Press.

Meyerhold, V. (ed. and trans. E. Braun) (1991) *Meyerhold on Theatre*, London: Methuen.

Opie, I. and Opie, P. (1988) *The Singing Game*, Oxford: Oxford University Press.

Petrobelli, P. (1994) *Music in the Theater*, Princeton: Princeton University Press.

Schoenberg, A. (ed. G. Strang) (1970) *Fundamentals of Musical Composition*, London: Faber & Faber.

Stanislavski, C. and Rumyantsev, P. (1998) *Stanislavski on Opera*, New York: Routledge.

Stanislavski, K. (1980) *An Actor Prepares*, London: Methuen.

Steane, J. (1996) 'But did they act?', *BBC Music Magazine* 5, 3: 63–5.

Storr, A. (1993) *Music and the Mind*, London: HarperCollins.

Stravinsky, I. (1942) *Poetics of Music*, Cambridge, Massachusetts: Harvard University Press.

Syer, J. and Connolly, C. (1987) *Sporting Body Sporting Mind: An athlete's guide to mental training*, London: Simon & Schuster.

Tetrazzini, L. (1923) *How to Sing*, London: C. Arthur Pearson.

Tippett, M. (1959) *Moving into Aquarius*, London: Routledge.

Warren, R. (1995) *Opera Workshop: Studies in Understanding and Interpretation*, Aldershot: Scolar Press.

Index of games and exercises by title and destination